Leadership

It's Simply Complicated

Philip Brandt

WingSpan Press

Published in the United States and the United Kingdom

by WingSpan Press, Livermore, CA

The WingSpan name, logo and colophon are the trademarks of WingSpan Publishing.

Cover art and illustrations by Maggie Lowe, Artist and Graphic Designer, AAIM Employers' Association

Names: Brandt, Philip.
Title: Leadership : it's simply complicated / Philip Brandt.
Description: Livermore, CA : Wingspan Press, 2016.
Identifiers: LCCN 2016953961 | ISBN 978-1-59594-668-3 (hardcover) | ISBN 978-1-59594-596-9 (pbk.) | ISBN 978-1-59594-918-9 (Kindle ebook)
Subjects: LCSH: Leadership. | Management. | Organizational effectiveness. | BISAC: BUSINESS & ECONOMICS / Leadership. | BUSINESS & ECONOMICS / Management.
Classification: LCC HD57.7 .B73 2016 (print) | LCC HD57.7 (ebook) | DDC 658.001--dc23.
First edition 2016

Printed in the United States of America

www.wingspanpress.com

Library of Congress Control Number: 2016953961

1 2 3 4 5 6 7 8 9 10

Table of Contents

Preface

Why is it simply complicated?

I don't know anyone named Mike or Dave Stillwell. To the best of my knowledge, there is no company named Stillwell Distributors in the United States. However, that does not in any way mean the story you are about to read is purely fiction.

I have had the privilege of leading many high performing organizations in my career and consider myself fortunate to have worked with - and for - some of the world's very best leaders. More recently, I am in the unique and extremely rewarding position to lead an organization that serves a diverse group of 1600 employers. I see their challenges. I know their pain. Conversely, I am witness to their amazing accomplishments! And, I am truly grateful that they continually share their lessons learned and best practices.

However, there seems to be one common issue that affects all organizations, to some degree. Most leaders are exceptional with business processes, but some struggle with *people* processes. In the People-Process-Product equation, they often struggle most with the people side of the equation. They find it especially arduous *blending* the three dynamics together to achieve the desired business results.

In the last twenty years, countless books have been published on talent management methodologies. "It's Simply Complicated" brings a simple human capital solution for any organization to build a foundation on. It is a simple model of hiring, developing, and retaining the right people, with the right attitude and aptitude, in the most complex environments and organizations.

I am a strong proponent of the "promise" to your employees. It boldly proclaims your commitment to not only the organization, but to each individual employee. I have found that leaders from elite organizations around the world have successfully implemented their promise. Not surprisingly, these organizations typically outperform organizations that do not have a promise. It is my hope that someday, all organizations will have a "Promise" statement, in addition to their traditional Mission, Vision, and Value Proposition statements.

Philip Brandt

Foreword

When I first met Phil Brandt, I was immediately drawn to his winsome personality and his business brilliance. Phil has become a trusted friend and respected colleague, and after listening to his innovative ideas on how to build the greatest organization in the world, I encouraged him to write a book and share his breakthrough leadership strategies with everyone.

I have lost count of the number of "leadership" books I've read over the past fifty years. But, *Leadership: It's Simply Complicated* is one of best books I've ever read! You may be asking yourself, "Why do we need another book on leadership?" If you do a search on Amazon for "leadership," you'll be bombarded by more than 100,000 book titles on the subject. You might be tempted to think, "With so many books on leadership, there should be no leadership problems!"

However, Gallup's research reveals that leaders around the world aren't doing any better at engaging their people than they were 10 years ago. The data starkly underscores a dismal truth: we are still over-managed and under-led in every area of life. In spite of all those "how–to" books, we have a significant leadership deficit.

A great many of the books on leadership are too complicated; they overwhelm the reader who believes the contents are too complex to learn and too cumbersome to implement in his or her organization. What I love about *Leadership: It's Simply Complicated,* is its simplicity! Phil has masterfully demystified the intricacies of leadership. And, because the book is written in parable style, it is easy and enjoyable to follow Phil's leadership roadmap toward "systemic success," as he calls it.

Let me give you three compelling reasons why you should read *Leadership: It's Simply Complicated*:

(1) Phil Brandt gets it; he understands what it takes to build the greatest organization in the world as well as anyone I have ever read. Phil isn't just a great teacher and storyteller, although he certainly is those things; he is the consummate business builder, one who understands the pain points and roadblocks that all leaders encounter, and he succinctly explains how to eliminate that pain and overcome all the obstacles. Phil has actually applied these invaluable leadership lessons and used them to transform major organizations, including his own, AAIM Employers' Association.

(2) Too many leadership books fail to show the reader how to integrate the best human systems with the best business systems. But this is where *Leadership: It's Simply Complicated* does a remarkable job in emphasizing the importance of blending these two worlds together and providing leaders with a step-by-step leadership formula for making the integration of the best human systems and business systems a sustainable, systemic reality in their organization.

(3) Finally, I firmly believe that Phil has written the

definitive leadership manual for both young, aspiring leaders, and seasoned professionals. Phil has put all his years of education and experience into one wonderfully practical book, which is chock-full of practical, powerful business solutions that leaders can, and should, utilize in order to feel confident and competent about motivating others to willingly and passionately follow their leadership. I wish that someone had handed me this book when I first started my career; I would have avoided many of the pitfalls that beset so many young, emerging leaders... and so many experienced ones!

I am making *Leadership: It's Simply Complicated* required reading for all of my clients. This book is a much-needed contribution to the field of leadership development. I am so proud of Phil - not just for giving us an exceptional book on leadership, but for inspiring us with his passion for developing leaders and organizations!

Sincerely,
Jack Lannom
President and CEO
People First International

Chapter One
"My Business Is a Mess!"

Simply complicated. Driving down the interstate, Mike Stillwell reflects on the oxymoron his father so often referenced when he was a young man seeking solutions to the challenges of the business. It is a beautiful, golden October afternoon, the kind of day Mike's father used to call "football weather," but Mike takes no pleasure in it. Instead, he is deep in thought as he murmurs, "Simply complicated... simply complicated... simply complicated."

He remembers eight years ago when he first took over the business and thought it was going to be easy. Today it feels more like an all-day, every day migraine headache.

Mike heaves a tired sigh. For just a moment he takes his eyes off the road to glance at the vista of fall foliage. His eyes then shift back to the road ahead and he switches his cell phone into his left hand and dials his wife.

"Hi hun, how is everything going?" Lee Anne answers.

"I'm sorry I didn't get a chance to swing by the house to say goodbye to you and the kids," Mike says, genuinely disappointed. "Things are such a mess at work and I was already running late. I hate to be away all weekend. I honestly wish I could have told Uncle Dave, 'Sorry, can't help you,' but that wouldn't be right."

Mike checks the driver's mirror and swings his Explorer out into the passing lane to move ahead of a slower vehicle. After a short conversation with Lee Ann, Mike agrees, "Yes, you're right. We wouldn't just be letting Dave down, but Aunt Rita too. Well, I'll do my best to be home in time for dinner Sunday night. I love you, honey. Please tell the kids I love them...Bye."

In a warm voice Lee Ann says I love you and wishes him good luck.

After hanging up, Mike taps his phone a few times, selecting some upbeat music. The music relaxes him, and he settles back in the driver's seat for the remaining 50 miles before he arrives at his Uncle Dave's house. Mike ticks the cruise control up to travel a few miles per hour faster and then glances out the driver's window again, making a conscious effort to relax and enjoy the view.

His cell phone rings with the ring tone indicating the call is coming from his office. *It hasn't even been an hour since I got on the road, and they're calling already?* He shuts off the music and grabs his phone. "This is Mike," he says curtly.

"I'm sorry to bother you, Mike, but we've got a situation here."

Mike's lips purse with his unhappiness as he recognizes the voice of Luis Garcia, the second shift operations manager at his distribution business. "What's wrong, Luis?"

"Same problem we had last week. Three of our fork truck drivers are out, and Johnson and Williams called in. Askins has only been with us for three weeks; he's no call, no show."

"Well, he's done then," Mike says with finality. "If he comes back Monday, tell him he's gone. My *gosh!* People just have no *commitment* these days. This couldn't happen at a worse time!"

"I know. We're supposed to get those trucks out to Top Technical this afternoon, and it's not looking good."

"Whaddya mean? We *can't* drop the ball with Top Technical. They're our biggest customer!" Alarmed, Mike starts firing questions, stepping on the gas to pass another vehicle. "What have you done so far? Who's staying late from the first shift? Who have you called from third shift to come in early and work a double?"

"That's why I called you," Luis says evenly. "Only one guy from the morning crew was willing to stay. It's a Friday afternoon, and people have plans. I've called everybody on third shift. Out of ten forklift operators, only three answered. Two said 'No thanks.' Jerry Rhodes said he'd come in at five o'clock, but that doesn't do us much good. We're still down two drivers."

"*Only two guys* are willing to help?" Mike says, his

mounting frustration evident in his acid tone. "What's *wrong* with these people? Don't they realize how badly we'll be hurt if we lose the Top Technical account? They're already unhappy because we were four days late on their parts order last month. *Now this* order is a day behind. Don't our people realize losing this account will mean layoffs? If they don't give a rip about the company they work for, don't they care about their own *jobs?!"* Fear and anger are making Mike's voice unnaturally harsh.

"Boss, I'm sorry," Luis says softly. "I know this is a serious situation."

"*Serious!*" Mike rasps, his voice continuing to rise. "This is a potential *disaster!* Don't tell me you just gave up on this, Luis. Who's there right now who's qualified to operate the forks?"

"I thought of that too. You know we were training Diego Hernandez, but he resigned last month. Randy Gordon is qualified, but he put in for a personal day today over a month ago. He's on a hunting trip. So the reason I'm calling is—"

"And you're just letting me know this *now?* Luis, it's already mid-afternoon. Those trucks have *got* to go out *today!* Have you tried the temp agency?"

"That's why I'm calling," Luis says cautiously. "The last time this happened you told me never to authorize temps without checking with you first. So—"

"So call them, for Pete's sake!" Mike is practically

shouting now. He glances at his speedometer and realizes he is speeding so he backs off the gas pedal.

"I have," Luis replies calmly. "They can have two men here in an hour. I just need to get your authorization."

"An *hour?*" Mike groans at the delay. "Are you gonna get all those trucks out? I *can't* call Top Technical back again and tell them we're another day late."

"I think we'll be OK, Mike. I'm still calling the third shift drivers who haven't answered. I'm pretty sure I can get one more guy. It's gonna be tight, but we should have the trucks out."

"Well, make *sure* you get that guy," Mike says sourly. He takes a deep breath and releases it slowly. "OK," he says in a more normal tone. "Give me a call or a text at five o'clock to let me know where we stand."

"I will."

Mike hangs up the phone and flings it disgustedly onto the passenger's seat. "Calling for my authorization," he mutters.

Somehow it never occurs to him that Luis was doing *exactly* what Mike had instructed him to do just two months ago.

Mike Stillwell is of average height, always neatly dressed and well-groomed. His thick, dark hair shows signs of early greying. He takes pride in his physical appearance and is most comfortable in a pair of khakis and a polo shirt from his collection of many. When he was younger Mike had more time to keep fit, but over the years he has developed a slight middle-aged paunch due to a lack of regular exercise and late-night, hurried meals after a long day at work.

Most of all, Mike is a problem-solver. It's his nature to attack problems and overcome them by the force of his experience, his wits, and his powerful personality. However, as he had confessed to his wife, Lee Anne, not 20 minutes ago, the problems at his distribution company are starting to feel unmanageable and overwhelming.

Mike formally succeeded his father as the CEO of Stillwell Distributors eight years ago when his father died suddenly. At that time, the company employed a total of 55 people, keeping two shifts very busy receiving, storing, and shipping products, primarily components for technology companies. Stillwell Distributors had an extremely small advertising budget and a tiny sales force. That model was working well; however, because Mike's father had established a tremendous reputation for integrity and efficiency, new business almost seemed to take care of itself.

Mike has never worked for any other company. As a kid he spent hours running up and down the long rows of racks, climbing up and down them the way his childhood friends climbed trees. Watching in awe as the forklift drivers zipped up and down the rows, some bringing cartons and crates to be stored, others working busily to load the trucks that lined up in the yard as early as 3:00 a.m. in order to be "first in, first out." When Mike was thirteen, he drove a fork truck for the first time, and what had been a childlike interest in the distribution business solidified into a lifelong love.

At 16, Mike had wanted nothing more than to quit high school and go to work full time in the bustling distribution center, but his father was adamant: not only would Mike finish high school, but he would get a four-year degree in business administration at the state university. Mike's father had started working full time at age 15; he was determined that his son was going to get the education he never did.

Mike remembers his dad saying, "I truly am grateful you want to come to work with me, but you're going to be so much more valuable to the organization when you learn all the new ways to do business. I'm just an old warehouse man; you're going to be the CEO of a corporation. I need you to prepare for that, just like a soldier goes through boot camp and then advanced training. Will you do that for me, son?"

Mike loved his father and had readily agreed, working summers at the distribution center and finally graduating with honors. Then, with his father's delighted consent, Mike went one step further and earned his MBA in two years, finally coming to work full time at Stillwell Distributors 24 years ago. Mike was bursting with new ideas that he had gained from his time at the university, which occasionally caused friction with his father, who resisted Mike's ideas for expansion and modernization.

"Son, I'm proud that you've learned so much about how to grow the business, and I'm sure it's going to be useful," his dad would say. "However, I'm not ready to take the business in that direction... yet. But when you do, I want you to think about this: I have a system in place that has kept 50 families well taken care of for many years, through good times and bad. There's no one more trusted and respected in our field than Stillwell Distributors. Most of our new customers have been referred to us by one of our happy customers. Mike, I like the way that system works. When the time comes to expand the business, we'll need to ensure we don't drift away from our people systems."

Mike initially chafed at his father's intractability, but he bided his time. He appreciated how the entire staff genuinely loved his father and recognized that the current business model was working very well. Meanwhile, Mike's dad continued to groom him for leadership. Mike had to earn every promotion, but those promotions came: lead stacker, lead driver, a year in the maintenance department so that he could learn how to keep the equipment running, two years in sales, back to the warehouse floor as a shift supervisor, two years as the third shift operations manager, and then, finally, general manager.

During this period, Mike married Lee Anne Russello, whom he had known since high school. Lee Anne knew exactly what she was getting into when she said "Yes." She was pursuing her own career path, working as an assistant professor at the state university, and she recognized that Mike was a high achiever who would never be content working a nine to five job. Over the years, she and Mike balanced the often competing demands of their careers to raise their two children.

Lee Anne worked hard to provide a happy, comfortable

home, never complaining about Mike's grinding schedule. Once in a while she would gently remind him that he was spending too little time with the kids, and Mike would dutifully—and, to his credit, not unhappily—devote more time to his family.

One of the family's favorite activities was taking the two-hour drive "to the country" to visit Mike's Uncle Dave, Mike's father's only brother. Dave Stillwell had worked in landscaping all his life and had done well enough to buy a beautiful five-acre parcel of land on a small, spring-fed pond. Dave had built a cottage there, nestled in the shade of five towering pines, and settled in.

Several years ago, Dave's wife of 30 years died suddenly of a massive cerebral hemorrhage, and Dave never remarried. Mike sometimes wondered how Dave managed to do so well. His landscaping business couldn't be very prosperous, Mike reasoned, because Dave was never too busy with work that he couldn't make time for Mike's family to visit, even on short notice. This was often the case due to Mike's work schedule and somewhat impulsive nature. Mike, Lee Anne, and the children usually spent about three long weekends a year and a week in the summer packed into Dave's cottage, "camping out," as they called it, taking turns sleeping on the couch and on air mattresses, fishing in the pond, enjoying long walks in a nearby forest, playing dominoes and other board games at night, and drinking in the quiet of the country. Some of Mike's happiest memories were centered in Dave's small, comfortable home.

The years flew by, punctuated by sorrow and joy… the passing of Mike's mother and Lee Anne successfully completing her grueling tenure review process. Mike's responsibilities at work continued to expand. While Mike was not yet called the CEO, his dad was working less and less and giving Mike more and more responsibility. Mike was confident that when his father retired, he was ready to assume the role of CEO and begin building on the solid foundation his dad had laid.

Mike remembers that morning eight years ago when he learned his father had died quietly in his sleep at age 72.

No one would ever suggest that Mike Stillwell had been born with a silver spoon in his mouth. He had worked hard all his life and endured many of life's setbacks and disappointments, but the death of his dad was the low point. He had loved his father deeply, even when he vigorously disagreed with him on company policy. Mike had somehow imagined that his dad would always be there to talk to and offer advice when Mike took over as CEO of Stillwell Distributors. Suddenly, Mike's best friend—his hero—was gone.

Immediately following the passing of Mike's father, the family took an extended vacation at Uncle Dave's cottage. Mike remembers Dave's quiet kindness. They sat up late into the night talking about grief and loss. In some subtle way, Dave and Mike's relationship changed during that visit from that of uncle/nephew to a solid, respectful friendship.

Unfortunately, after that visit Mike wound up seeing his Uncle Dave less and less. Mike shook off the sorrow of his father's passing and went to work to fulfill his vision for growing Stillwell Distributors. He was the owner now. He worked hard, worked his people hard, and the effort paid off. In eight short years, the company had virtually doubled in size, expanding to 100 employees, running three full shifts around the clock, with an administrative staff of about 25 who supported the business.

Mike bought out a neighboring bank of warehouses, wincing slightly when he signed the papers for a massive capital loan, and pushed his sales force to write more business to pay for the expansion. That new business came, but with it came a whole new set of challenges. Stillwell Distributors' receivables jumped significantly, but so did debt, labor costs, and expenses; profit margins were actually much thinner than they had been just a few years ago.

In recent years, when Lee Anne suggested getting away for some family time, Mike increasingly felt obligated to say things like, "Maybe in a couple of months, honey. We're just too busy at work right now."

Mike's cell phone trills with the "work" ringtone again, interrupting his thoughts. Recognizing he's still 30 minutes from Dave's cottage, he answers, fully expecting Luis Garcia to be on the line with an update.

"Yeah, Luis, how's it coming?" Mike says, hoping for good news.

"It's Janet actually," a woman's voice answers. Janet Scarborough is Stillwell Distributors' Human Resources Manager. Bright, hardworking, wholly dedicated to the success of Stillwell Distributors, Janet is one of Mike's most trusted leaders.

Mike's stomach tightens. He knows Janet doesn't normally call to chat about day-to-day affairs. "What's wrong, Janet?"

"I'm sorry to bother when you're on your way to your uncle's cottage, but I thought you'd want to hear about this right away: Ray Weir just gave his two weeks' notice."

Mike's grip on the steering wheel tightens as he keeps his eyes carefully fixed on the highway. Ray Weir is Stillwell Distributors' maintenance manager, the "Mr. Fix It" guy who keeps the fork trucks, powered pallet stackers, and everything else mechanical functioning.

Mike releases a heavy sigh. "Janet, please tell me you're kidding. Ray's been with us for what, fifteen years?"

"It would have been seventeen years next month," Janet says softly. "I wish I *was* joking. There aren't many people I would call 'irreplaceable,' but this hurts. Ray has always been a hard worker. I always believed he was incredibly loyal, and everyone says he's just magic with machinery. I don't imagine that someone with his ability will be easy to replace."

"What's going on with him? Have you talked to him?"

"Yes. Turns out Leland Distribution made him an offer

he couldn't refuse. He has coveted skills as a maintenance engineer and manager. We've always paid him at the high end of our scale, and Ray told me he's always been happy with his pay. That's not the issue. You know he's been working hard. A lot of times he's coming in seven days a week. Sometimes he fills in on the fork trucks when we need him, coming in in the middle of the night, and so on. Now he's got another job that pays him $500 a month more, and they promised him no more than 50 hours a week."

"$500 dollars *a month* more! How in the world can Leland afford to pay him that?" Mike says plaintively. "I swear, they pay *everybody* on their staff a lot more than we do. How can we compete with *that?*"

"He said it wasn't the money, Mike. I asked him what it would take to keep him. Obviously he's happy to get such a big raise, but he said he's just gotten frazzled working for us. He's exhausted from running around, putting out fires, and he's starting to forget what his family looks like."

Mike shakes his head, drumming his fingers on the steering wheel. "I can certainly relate to that," he murmurs, almost to himself.

"So can I," Janet agrees.

Mike stiffens. "You too? Are you feeling overwhelmed?"

"Oh, no, that's not what I meant," Janet says quickly. "You know me, I *like* being so busy. But I know there are...other people who probably feel like Ray."

"Anybody I should know about? This is a real gut-punch for us!"

"You know I would tell you if I knew something. Unfortunately, there are those times I don't find out until it's too late, like with Ray. But you hear people talking. You can tell they're stressed."

"*I'm* stressed," Mike quietly admits. "The last few years, it seems like every time we turn around we're losing somebody else we can't afford to lose."

"Again, Mike, I'm sorry to call you with bad news when you're headed out for a long weekend. I thought you'd want to know right away."

"Yes, thank you, you were right to call," Mike readily agrees. "This is actually a working weekend. My Uncle Dave's building an addition onto his cottage. His sister, my Aunt Rita, has been diagnosed with Parkinson's disease, and Dave wants her to live with him so he can look after her. A lot of friends and family have pitched in to help with the construction, and this weekend is my turn." Mike shakes his head. "It sure turned out to be a bad time to be away from the office."

Mike slumps back into the driver's seat, brooding and worried. *I should have told Uncle Dave I couldn't come,* he thinks sourly. *My business is a mess! We're late on our deliveries. We don't seem to be able to hire people who want to do anything more than just pick up a paycheck. I remember Dad talking about how important it is to hire the right people and have the right people processes. It sure doesn't seem like I've been doing a good job of that. Look at the mess with the fork drivers!*

His impatience rising, Mike maneuvers his Explorer around a slow moving car. *I swear, people just don't have the work ethic they used to have! They aren't responsible, they don't show up to work, half the time they don't even call in, and they have no sense of loyalty. The few good ones we have—some of the best people that Dad hired, like Ray Weir—are moving over to the competition, and a lot of the folks Dad hired are getting older. They just don't work as fast as they used to!*

Once again, Mike's fingers are drumming nervously on the steering wheel. *Customers keep telling me they want more from us, but instead we're giving them less. They want on-time deliveries, and our current delivery problems are causing us to lose some of our most profitable accounts...companies that Dad had built such solid relationships with.*

Mike almost unconsciously eases his Explorer over into the exit lane. His mind is wrestling with the problems that seem to batter his company almost nonstop. *I doubled the size of the company in the last eight years, but it seems like I've quadrupled the headaches. When Dad was building the company, he did a lot of business on a handshake. You can't trust* anybody *today to do that! These big companies think nothing of muscling you around because they have the budgets and legal departments with some attack dog lawyer just waiting to rip somebody like me to pieces. They'd put me out of business and not think twice about it.*

By now Mike is just minutes from Uncle Dave's cottage, and his mind jumps to the task ahead. *I should feel happy to be coming here to help out. Dave has always been so kind to us. I'll never forget that night we sat up talking about how much I was missing Dad. It never occurred to me that he missed him just as much! Hearing him talk about his wife dying and how he still misses her…I don't know what I'd do without Lee Anne.*

Mike drives slowly down a narrow, two-lane road. Tall red maples line either side, their leaves shining in the afternoon sunlight, beautiful auburn and gold shades, create a golden tunnel to drive through, yet Mike does not see them. His mind is too busy wrestling with unpleasant thoughts. *I love Dave a lot. With Dad and Mom gone, he's probably the closest person to me after Lee Anne and the kids. It stinks we haven't gotten out here more to visit. He's retired and living the life, while my own business has me working harder than ever! I thought it would be easier, but instead it just presents one worry after another. I've done a great job growing the business, but a poor job of managing the growth!*

Now, Dave needs help putting the roof on the new addition. He can't do it himself because of his bad hip, and he's got to get the cottage closed in before winter. If I was a good person, I'd be coming up here at least once a month to help with the work. Instead I've been dragging my feet and wishing I didn't have to do it at all.

Without realizing it, Mike has been driving ever more slowly. He can see the towering oak tree that is the landmark for Dave's driveway. It is almost as if Mike doesn't want to arrive at his destination. He simply does not know how he is going to put on a happy face for his uncle.

The "work" ringtone sounds again. Mike winces, as if feeling a sudden, stabbing pain. He pulls the Explorer over to the side of the road, shoves the shifter into Park, and picks up the phone.

"This is Mike." His voice is low, ominous. He does *not* want to hear any more bad news this day!

"Mike, this is Brad Harrington."

Brad is Stillwell Distributors' national sales manager. Mike's voice brightens. "Brad, I'll bet you're calling to tell me you closed that one big firm in Arkansas. What's their name again?"

"I'm afraid not." Brad's deep voice usually sounds bold and confident, but today he sounds disappointed. "I've got some bad news."

"I've already had *lots* of bad news today." The impatient tone is back in Mike's voice.

Brad hesitates before responding. "Unfortunately we were two days late with this week's delivery to Lancaster. They say they're done with us. They're pulling all their stock."

Mike's eyes flare open. "Two *days* late! That delivery went out Tuesday...on time! You told me so yourself. What *happened?*"

"It *did* go out on Tuesday," Brad affirms, "but Shipping made a mistake. Somehow the trucks were routed to Illinois, not Iowa. We didn't find out until late yesterday afternoon."

"So why didn't you *tell* me late yesterday afternoon?" Mike barks.

Brad hesitates, knowing that Mike will not like his answer. "I…I didn't want to tell you what had happened until I could tell you we had it solved."

"I guess you didn't solve it too well," Mike growls, "if they want to pull their stock!"

"We got the shipment turned around, hired some extra drivers, and it unloaded at noon today. I stayed in close touch with Ed Stearns at Lancaster throughout the entire process. He sounded pretty irritated, as you'd expect, but I thought he would calm down. I was planning to call him tomorrow to follow up and apologize again, but he just called with this news."

Mike is so angry that he is breathing heavily, like a man who just ran a race. He opens his mouth once, twice, three times, to tell Brad what a disaster this is, how unacceptable this latest mistake is, that Brad should clean out his desk right now.

Mike closes his eyes and makes a deliberate effort to control his temper. He thumps his closed fist against his thigh. When he finally speaks again, his voice is very soft. "Is Ed in his office now?"

"I just hung up with him three minutes ago. But Mike, he told me to tell you not to even bother contacting him. He said, 'Don't insult me by calling me and offering some discount to try and keep my business. We're through.' He's sending trucks on Tuesday to pick up their stock. He doesn't even want us to do that final delivery."

Mike can see Stillwell Distributors' list of receivables in his mind's eye. This is a significant loss—not a crippling one, but a significant setback. "I'll try calling Ed Monday morning and see if there's anything I can do to salvage this." Mike pauses. "Brad, you don't need me to tell you that something like this must never, *ever* happen again."

Brad realizes that his job is hanging by a thread. "I understand, Mike. I'm truly very sorry."

Mike replies quietly, "I know," and hangs up the phone. He rests his elbows on the Explorer's steering wheel and puts his face in his hands. He wants to be a good leader. He cares deeply about those who report to him, but sometimes it's hard and he can't hide from the facts.

Mike shakes his head slowly back and forth; his stomach actually aches with stress. He then begins to realize and admit to himself that much of the blame for his managers' poor performance rests on his own shoulders.

Still sitting idle on the side of the road, Mike lifts his head and stares blankly for a moment. He feels empty, beaten. For about the twentieth time this week, he considers picking up his phone and telling Uncle Dave that he can't make it, even though Dave's cottage is now just 200 yards away. Mike heaves a deep, desolate sigh. "C'mon, Mike," he says softly. "You've gotten enough wrong today. Let's do something right."

His cell phone vibrates, signifying an incoming text message. Mike looks at his phone with an expression of fear and revulsion. Slowly, almost unwillingly, Mike picks up his phone. The message is from Luis Garcia:

All is well with Top Technical. We're finishing up the last trucks now.

Relief seeps through him and Mike quickly types a reply:

Way to go! Did you get more third shift guys in?

After a moment, the reply comes back:

No luck there, but we got those two temps and I shifted some people off the Bowling Green delivery. We have some flexibility on that order, so we'll have everything out on time."

"Well," Mike says aloud, "Top Technical is still a day late, but that can't be helped now." He wants to leave Luis feeling positive, so he types:

Good job, Luis ☺. That delivery HAD to go today and you made it happen! Thank you.

After a moment, his phone buzzes again:

Sorry I gave you heartburn, boss!

"It's not just you giving me heartburn, Luis," Mike murmurs, but he replies:

Nothing a few antacids won't cure! ☺ Thanks again.

Crisis averted, Mike thinks, but there is no sense of happiness, or even satisfaction. At least the ache in his stomach has stopped. *If we'd lost the Lancaster account and Top Technical in the same day...that might have meant lights out for us.*

The sun is sinking down behind the trees lining the rural road, and the gathering dusk perfectly mirrors Mike's mood. He drops the Explorer into gear and eases down the road, taking a right onto the gravel driveway sheltered by the big oak. After traveling thirty feet, the driveway bends to the right, and the cottage, which is completely hidden from the main road, comes into view. Mike's eyes widen and he stops the SUV.

"Oh no!" he says aloud, dismayed.

Mike knows enough about building to see that there is a great deal of work to do. Dave is not adding a single room to the cottage; he is expanding the entire structure. There is a stack of roof joists to hang, plywood to cut and nail in place, and tar paper and shingles to affix to the roof. Mike had promised Dave that he wouldn't leave until the roof is on over the addition and the shingles done, but somehow Mike had convinced himself that this would be a quick and easy job.

His mind is racing. *We're gonna have to bust it just to get done this weekend! I told Lee Anne, I'd be home for dinner Sunday. I'll be lucky to get home in time to say goodnight to the kids! This is a* huge *job!*

Mike shakes his head emphatically. Suddenly overwhelmed he reaches for the Explorer's shifter to drop it in reverse and back out of the driveway.

Just at that moment, a tall, lean man steps out from behind the stack of roof joists. Even at this distance, Mike recognizes his Uncle Dave. His face lighting up with a big grin, Dave waves both his arms at Mike, imitating an airport ground crewman waving a plane to its docking point.

Once again, waves of guilt wash over Mike. Was he really about to turn around and drive home? Slowly, evenly he reminds himself: *This man has always been there for you. He's never once asked you for a thing. It's not his fault you've lost your way with the business. Now figure out how to put a genuine smile on your face…and go get this done!*

Glancing at his reflection in the rearview mirror, Mike gives a firm nod, takes a deep breath, and continues driving toward Dave's cottage.

Cottage Takeaways

- Mike finds himself caught up in a series of common challenges that most leaders face every day.
- He does not yet recognize that these challenges are systemic in nature and the “breakdowns” are a direct result of a lack of people processes.
- Since he is a problem solver and does not have a solution, he is reacting with an emotional response.
- These problems are interfering with his personal life.
- He feels alone, frustrated, and responsible.

Chapter Two
"One Last Chance"

Seven o'clock Saturday morning finds Dave and Mike standing outside the cottage, both men holding steaming mugs of coffee.

Friday night had passed quickly. As he had done so often when Mike's family came to visit, Dave had cooked steaks and ears of corn on an outdoor grill. It has been more than a year since Mike's last visit, and he is beginning to realize how much he has missed his uncle's company. Dave is a warm, friendly man and a good conversationalist.

Slowly Mike felt the tension drain away. He had thought he and Dave might spend the night working under flood lights to get a jump on the construction. In fact, when Dave started to fire up the grill, Mike had asked if they wouldn't do better getting right to work.

Dave had turned to Mike with a broad smile. "Work? Tonight? No way! We'll get our work done in plenty of time." Dave looked mischievously at Mike, his brown eyes twinkling. "I didn't bring you up here to work your tail off, Mike. I've been looking forward to catching up with you!"

With that, Dave had popped open two bottles of beer, handed Mike a frosted mug from the freezer, and the two men sat on the front porch in wooden rocking chairs watching the final rays of the sun setting over the pond. The night air was crisp and the evening sky a deep, rich blue. Dave kept the conversation moving, asking questions and listening to Mike with genuine interest. Mike leaned back in the rocker, enjoying the night air and the tantalizing aroma of the steaks grilling, and talked about Lee Anne's work at the university, their children, and the St. Louis Cardinals' recently concluded season.

Mike had dreaded the question he was sure would come— "So how's your business doing?"—but somehow, with all the questions Dave asked about Mike's world, that one hadn't come up.

Later they had moved inside the cottage to eat a delicious dinner. The two men agreed to make an early start the next day, and Mike, who often has difficulty sleeping these days, had slept like a baby.

Now, in the bright early morning light, as the two men survey the task at hand, Mike starts to feel stirrings of anxiety again. "Dave," he says, "I don't know how we're going to get all this work done. I feel like I should have come up on Thursday."

Dave sips his coffee, then shakes his head, feigning

sorrow. "Oh, ye of little faith. I told you last night I didn't bring you up here to work you to death. Don't underestimate your poor old uncle."

Mike chuckles, flushing slightly. "I'm sorry. We didn't talk about the business last night, but I'm really busy at work. I just can't afford to stay an extra day to finish this."

Dave shakes his head, smiling. "Mike, truly, there's nothing to worry about."

As if on cue, Mike's cell phone emits the "work" ringtone. Mike's stomach tightens, and he looks apologetically at his uncle. "I'm sorry. Usually I'm at the office on Saturday." He manages a weak grin. "I guess some folks are a little lost without me."

Mike swings away to answer. "This is Mike," he says quietly into the phone.

"Hi Mike, it's Janet. I hope I'm not calling you too early."

"That's OK." Mike glances at his watch. "What's wrong?"

"I got a text message from the first shift operations manager, and I thought you'd want to know about this right away. We sent two stackers home on suspension."

"What happened this time?" Mike asks, irritation twisting his gut.

"I wasn't there, but the lead stacker said that one of the guys was playing a radio and another guy didn't like his musical selection. One guy likes rap and the other likes country, or something like that."

"What were they doing listening to the radio in the first place?" Mike asks sharply. "The rules are crystal clear about that."

"It's Saturday, Mike," Janet replies. "We let them listen to music on the weekend."

"Ah," Mike grunts. "I forgot." He thinks for a moment. "So it's a two-day suspension?"

"Yes, that's right. I know we're short on staff, but this had to be done. There were no punches thrown, but apparently that's only because a couple of people got in between them before that could happen. I'm told they were pretty much nose-to-nose, shouting and swearing."

"OK, Janet, I appreciate you letting me know. Maybe we'll just have to ban music all together."

"I thought you might say that," Janet replies. "That's why I called. I know this could've waited, but I was hoping you might give it some thought over the weekend. Then maybe we could talk about the situation some more on Monday morning. I think this event is just a symptom of a deeper problem. We have a lot of cultural differences, and it seems like more and more they're boiling over into some kind of unpleasantness. I don't think it's about music; it goes deeper than that.

The radio was just the flash point."

"Yes," Mike agrees with resignation. "I'm sure you're right. Thanks again."

"Before you go," Janet says quickly, "don't forget we have that OFCCP meeting Monday."

"O-F-*who?*"

"OFCCP," Janet says patiently. "Office of Federal Contract Compliance Programs."

"The Feds again?" Mike shakes his head impatiently.

"Yes, it's about compliance issues."

Mike groans. "Janet, I'm awfully busy!"

"There's no way to avoid this," Janet says firmly. "We've got these government contracts, so we *must* undergo this audit. You know that if we're not in compliance with federal affirmative action guidelines, we could be in danger of losing our government contracts. I need you there for the meeting, Mike."

"I'll be there, this is important to me," Mike assures her, then ends the call.

He stares out over the pond. A pleasant breeze is blowing, and the rising sun causes the water to reflect an iridescent brilliance, yet he takes no pleasure in the beautiful vista.

One thing after another, he bemoans. *It's not just people and vendors and customers, I've got the government telling me who to hire, how many, and how much to pay them!*

"Trouble at work?" Dave asks, concern in his voice.

Mike turns to Dave and nods, the edges of his mouth curved in a frown. "Yeah, two guys wanted to fight over which radio station to listen to." Mike looks thoughtfully down at the ground for a moment. "My HR manager says it's a matter of workplace demographics, and I'm sure she's right."

Mike raises his gaze to meet Dave's. "You know, when I was a kid, everyone on the workforce had a lot in common. Just about everyone was white, they were all men, almost all of them had grown up in the Midwest—shoot, a lot of them went to the same high school! Everybody rooted for the Cardinals."

Mike shakes his head. "Today, we've got a very diverse workplace. A full third of our workforce is women. We've got people from Mexico, Brazil, Portugal, even a guy from China and a woman from Russia. We've got all generations and some people who speak little or no English."

Dave's bright brown eyes are focused on his nephew's face as he speaks. "That's a challenge, all right," he says, his tone sympathetic.

Mike laughs weakly. "I guess you didn't have to deal with that so much out here in the country."

"You might be surprised," Dave says. "Creating a strong internal culture doesn't just happen. It takes focused action."

"Yeah." Mike is looking back down at the ground, not really listening. He doesn't expect his uncle, who ran a landscaping business out of the back of a couple of pickup trucks, to understand the intricacies of managing a national distribution hub.

Dad didn't really have the same kind of complexity in his workforce, Mike broods silently. *Dad and Dave were from a different generation. Gosh, business has changed so much in the last fifteen years or so.* For a moment he mentally reviews the broad spectrum of humanity employed by Stillwell Distributors, all of them depending on him to make good decisions for the future of the business. Mike's lips tighten. *Doesn't seem like I've been making many good decisions lately,* he muses bitterly. *I want to do well for our people...not just for my family, but for our employees, too. They're counting on me!*

Mike gradually becomes aware that his uncle is watching him closely and he shakes his head, trying to clear away the negative thoughts. "Just a little distracted, Dave. I'm ready to go."

Dave grins...and Mike's phone rings again. Mike's eyes widen in disbelief, and he holds the phone out away from him, staring at it disgustedly. He glances at Dave. "Maybe my HR manager forgot to tell me something?" Mike's voice is almost plaintive.

He taps the phone. "This is Mike."

"Debbie Williams, Mike."

Debbie is the operations manager on the first shift. "Good morning, Debbie," Mike says, trying to keep his tone pleasant.

"We've got an issue. I know you don't like surprises, so I wanted to call you right away."

"That's OK," Mike assures her. "Janet just called me about the fight over the radio."

"I know. That's not why I called."

Mike's heart sinks at Debbie's ominous words. "What's the problem?"

"One of our newest fork truck drivers smashed into a rack and a palette fell. We've got some damaged product."

"Anyone hurt?" Mike quickly asks, worried about his employees.

"No, everyone's OK. Just a young, inexperienced driver trying to do too much too quickly. But the palette that fell was part of the D & N Instruments order that's scheduled to go out today. We have no replacement parts."

"Oh come *on!"* Mike says, his words coming out on a savage groan. "So now *that* order is going to be incomplete?"

"I'm afraid so."

"Well, call Brad Harrington. He likes to sleep in on Saturday mornings, but you keep calling until he answers. Tell him I said to take charge of this personally, Debbie, do you understand? I don't care who the sales rep is. I want Brad to make the call to D & N himself and get this smoothed over. Right away!"

"Yes, sir," Debbie responds. "I'll call him right now."

"You tell that driver to climb down off that lift and start hand-picking orders!" Mike snaps. "I don't want him within a hundred feet of a forklift. Have you got that?"

"But Mike, he's actually one of our better workers—"

"No 'buts.' Get him off that truck!" Mike doesn't wait for a reply. Instead he stabs at his phone repeatedly with his index finger to end the call. He looks out at the sparkling pond again, wondering how many times he could make the phone skip across the top of the water if he gave it a good fling.

All of a sudden Mike abruptly spins around and glares at Dave. "My *gosh*! You can't count on *anybody* to get *anything* right!" He waves the phone, almost accusingly, at his uncle. "This thing hasn't stopped ringing since I left the office yesterday. It *never* stops ringing! One problem after another after *another* and *nobody* has the ability to think for themselves. Dave, they can't solve the problems they created, much less anticipate a problem and prevent it."

Dave is listening and nodding with understanding. "I remember feeling that way about my own business...like it was running me, instead of me running the business."

"Yeah?" Mike realizes his voice is thick with sarcasm, but he is too angry to care. "Well, when you have some ideas about how to run a major distribution center, I'd be happy to hear them!"

Something flashes in Dave's eyes and then quickly disappears. "I might have some ideas, Mike," he says mildly, "but I don't think you'd be interested in hearing them."

Mike realizes that his thoughtless remark had stung. He takes a deep breath and steps closer to Dave. "I'm sorry," Mike says raggedly. "Please forgive me for snapping like that. I'm just under a lot of stress at work."

"Apology accepted." Dave waves away Mike's words. "Don't give it another thought. Honestly, I'm thinking it's me who should apologize to *you*. It looks like I dragged you out here to the woods when you need to be giving your full attention to your business. My timing is pretty bad."

Dave's kind words dissolve Mike's frustration. He shakes his head with genuine remorse. "It's not you, Dave; it's not your fault. I've just...got an awful lot on my plate." He glances around the yard at all the building materials and sighs. "And I have to admit to you, I don't have the slightest idea how just the two of us are going to get all this work done."

Dave feigns a wounded expression. "I am deeply hurt by your lack of confidence in me," he mocks.

Mike can't help but chuckle at the humor in his uncle's eyes. "OK, Uncle Dave, reassure me," Mike says. He gestures toward the stack of roof trusses. "Seriously, we've got to manhandle all these trusses up top and set them in place. No offense, but I know your hip doesn't let you go scrambling up and down a ladder. I'm thinking this is gonna take us the better part of today."

Dave's brown eyes are twinkling. "'Man-handle.'" He looks up at the sky as if appealing to the heavens. "'Manhandle,' he says!" Dave then looks back at Mike with a wry expression. "I stopped manhandling things a long time ago."

Mike cocks his head to the side, confused. "Then how…?"

Dave glances at his watch. "The reason we're sitting here sipping coffee, Mike, instead of 'scrambling up and down ladders,' as you say, is because of the wonders of modern technology." His voice is dry. "You're familiar with the term 'boom truck,' yes?"

"Of course!" Mike knows that a boom truck operator could easily lift the roof trusses, one by one, up to the top of Dave's cottage, where he and Dave can quickly attach them. With a boom truck, the job that Mike had imagined would take all day will easily be completed in just a few hours.

Mike looks at Dave, his expression sheepish. "You have a boom truck coming?"

Dave grins and gives an exaggerated nod. "As a matter of fact, it'll be here in about five minutes, and I'm sure you noticed the scaffolding surrounding the new construction?"

Mike feels like a child being taught to tie his shoes, but Dave's good humor is so infectious that Mike can't help but chuckle at his own ignorance. "That's there so you won't have to scramble up and down a ladder?"

"You bet!" Dave says with great satisfaction. "With my bad hip, I *hate* climbing ladders. So what do you say we walk over to the cottage and I'll explain the 21st Century process for installing roof trusses?"

Mike nods humbly and grins back. "I'd like to learn, Uncle Dave."

By 10:30 that morning, the trusses are all settled firmly in place. Dave and Mike climb down from the scaffolding and thank the driver and his helper. Dave hands each man an envelope with a smile. "There's a little extra for coming out here on a Saturday," he says, tossing a teasing grin Mike's way. "Believe me, you took a great load off my nephew's mind!"

Mike grins along with the boom truck driver and shakes his head. "I don't think my uncle is going to let me live this one down!"

The driver laughs. "Live and learn," he says heartily

and climbs up into the truck's cab. "Thanks again, Mr. Stillwell," he calls to Dave.

Dave and Mike both turn and look up at the cottage. "How are you feeling now, Mike?" Dave asks. "Think we'll get it done?"

Mike opens his mouth to reply with a cheerful affirmative, but then his cell phone rings. He looks wearily at Dave. "Yeah, if this thing will stop ringing. Excuse me for a minute." He taps the cell phone and takes a few steps away toward the pond. "This is Mike."

"Hi Mike, it's Brad."

Mike's eyes narrow. "Is everything straightened out with D & N Instruments?"

"I *wish* that was why I was calling. Mike, I've got really bad news."

"What?" A chill creeps into Mike's voice.

"Luis Garcia called me 30 minutes ago," Brad begins explaining. "You know how they were scrambling yesterday to get the order out to Top Technical. He ended up pulling some guys off another job to help get Top Technical out on time. Well, those guys weren't familiar with our quality control process, and some product got left behind."

Mike grimaces because there has been a series of mistakes and late deliveries that have plagued service to Top Technical during the past year. Mike has called Sarah Short, Top Technical's vice president of operations, twice in the last six months to personally apologize.

"Have you called the customer to update them?" Mike asks.

"Yes, I called them right away. Five minutes ago, Sarah Short called back to tell me not to bother sending the missing product." Brad pauses, then his voice takes on a gloomy note as he continues, "She says they're finished with Stillwell."

The color drains from Mike's face. "Finished? What do you mean, 'finished'?"

"They're going to pull their business."

Mike freezes. For just a moment, time seems to stand still. "Brad," he says softly, "that could put us out of business. Top Technical is our largest account."

"I know, Mike."

"We'd have to lay off half our employees if we lose them, maybe more!"

"Yes." Brad's voice sounds very far away.

"I'll call Sarah right now," Mike says curtly. He hangs up his phone and starts scrolling through his contacts. He glances up at Dave, barely seeing him, his mind swirling with the ramifications of this news. "I'm sorry, Dave, this may take a few minutes. We've got a crisis."

Dave has heard Mike's half of the conversation with Brad, and his eyes are narrowed with concern. "Take all the time you need. I'll go make some sandwiches."

It takes Mike a full twenty minutes of abject pandering to mollify an icy Sarah Short. At first, Sarah holds firm on her decision to close Top Technical's account with Stillwell Distributors. Mike paces back and forth in Dave's yard, trying to keep the sheer desperation he is feeling out of his voice. He reminds Sarah of the long relationship between their two companies and offers to make massive cost concessions on the next two shipments—concessions which will force Stillwell Distributors to operate at a significant loss.

Finally, Sarah grudgingly concedes to accept the delivery of the missing product, keeping the account open "for now." She concludes the conversation with virtually the same warning Mike had issued to Brad Harrington the previous day. "Mike, this is the second time we have overlooked a grievous error on the part of your organization. There will not be a third time. Do you understand?"

"I understand," Mike says, feeling chastened. "No more mistakes."

"Frankly, Mike, I would have ended our relationship with any other vendor who displayed this kind of incompetence."

The seriousness in Sarah's voice has the ache in Mike's stomach flaring into fiery pain. "I understand," he repeats. He feels like a grade-schooler being scolded by the principal, but what else can he do? "I'm truly grateful for your kindness, Sarah."

"It's not about kindness," Sarah says brusquely. "I have a responsibility to my own organization. I don't know if you've given this any thought at all, Mike, but your mistakes make *me* look incompetent. I don't *like* looking incompetent. Not one bit."

In spite of his anxiety, Mike can feel anger rising. Sarah Short is rubbing his nose in his mess. But the survival of his company is at stake, so Mike keeps his voice level. "I'm truly sorry to have put you in a bad spot."

"*You're* the one who's in a bad spot, Mike," Sarah snaps. "Stillwell Distributors used to have such a great reputation for efficiency. That reputation is quite different now."

Mike's eyes squeeze shut. "I know."

"I hope you get it back, Mike." Sarah's authoritative tone has softened with genuine concern. "Your father was a good man, a *very* good man. I believe you are too, but you've certainly lost your way. I have never given another vendor this kind of grace, but because of the tremendous respect I had for your father—" the chill returns to Sarah's voice— "I'll give you this *one last* chance."

Mike feels like his throat is closing. "Thank you."

Then his phone beeps. Sarah Short has hung up.

Cottage Takeaways

- Stillwell Distributors does not have a robust process for people. This results in a systemic breakdown causing the business to perform poorly.
- Mike's reactionary decisions are not providing the infrastructure for long-term solutions.
- Like many business owners and leaders, Mike believes these problems are unique to his business.
- Mike believes only he can solve these problems.
- He does not recognize that his leadership team's behavior is a reflection of himself.

Chapter Three
"I'm in Over My Head!"

Mike stands stock still, looking out over the pond, seeing nothing. His mind is flashing through a kaleidoscopic whirl of images and sounds. He sees a forklift driver standing over a damaged palette of products, scratching his head in confusion...a group of employees lined up to punch out and go home before quitting time... the vacuous expressions of utterly uninspired workers. He hears voices uttering phrases such as, "It's late"..."It's wrong"..."I can't"..."I don't know how." And like a distant, ominous rumble of thunder, he hears the voice of Sarah Short decreeing: *This one last chance.* He is completely unaware that he is shaking his head from side to side and waving his arms in a helpless gesture of surrender.

My people don't know how to solve problems, Mike thinks bitterly, *and neither do I. I'm like the boy trying to plug up all the holes in the dam. I run from one hole to the next, but as soon as I get one hole plugged, POP! Another leak starts pouring water! You read all the time about how important it is to put the right people in place. Have I done such a terrible job of hiring? Or is it that I haven't put the right systems in place for them to operate?*

Mike's deep sigh catches in his throat. *Dad always used to say that the people who perform the work will usually have the best answers. Why don't I have any answers? The harder I work, the worse it gets.*

"Mike?"

Startled, Mike spins around. He was so deeply consumed by his despairing thoughts that he didn't hear Uncle Dave coming back out of the cottage.

"Dave, you surprised me!" Mike grins to cover his embarrassment.

"Sorry, I didn't mean to." Dave reaches a stack of plywood and sets down a tray filled with oversized sandwiches, bags of chips, two large cups packed with ice, and a pitcher of ice tea. He grins at Mike. "I don't want you going home and telling Lee Anne I worked you to death and didn't feed you. Dig in!"

Mike tries to smile and automatically reaches for one of sandwiches. It looks delicious, but his stomach is knotted so badly that he has absolutely no desire to eat.

Dave pours a cup of ice tea and hands it to Mike. Their eyes meet briefly and Mike looks quickly away, worried his internal pain and fear are stamped all over his face.

Dave sits on the stack of plywood and waves at an empty space next to him. "Take a load off."

Mike sits down gingerly next to Dave. Not wanting to hurt his uncle's feelings, he takes a bite of the sandwich. It tastes like cardboard. Mike's mouth is so dry that he's afraid he'll choke if he tries to swallow, so he takes a big swig of ice tea to wash it down. He can feel his uncle's eyes on his face and he looks away. He just doesn't feel like talking, and he is sure Dave is going to ask him about the long phone call with Sarah Short. *I'd love to be able to tell Sarah Short that she can take her last chance and—*

"So what do you think about the job now? Have we got a chance?"

Mike looks at Dave blankly. "The job?"

Dave points a thumb over his shoulder. "The cottage," he says with patience. "You were worried I was going to have you working until midnight tomorrow."

Mike refocuses and manages a tight grin. "Well, I'm feeling a lot better after the boom truck, but I don't think we're out of the woods yet." He taps his palm against the stacked sheets of plywood beneath him. "We're still going to have to cut these sheets of plywood to fit and nail them up there. I'm sure you're good with a saw, but all that's gonna eat up the rest of the day, for sure."

"No." Dave shakes his head. "It's all about taking a systemic approach to systemic success."

"You know, Dad used those phrases all the time— 'systemic approach' and 'systemic success.' I'm not sure I was listening as closely as I should have."

"Isn't that true of all of us when we were young?" Dave gives Mike a kindly smile. "I think what your dad was saying was that good planning and solid systems take stress and hurry out of your work, whatever that work might be."

Mike shrugs. "I know that's true. I'm still thinking that I should have planned to stay a day longer. Then we could have gotten the house done in plenty of time."

"Not a 'house,' Mike," Dave says, raising a cautionary finger in reproach. "We're building a *home* for Aunt Rita. Probably the last home she'll know in this life."

Mike nods, flushing slightly. "Yes, you're right, of course. A home."

"As for planning," Dave continues briskly, "if I had needed you to stay until Monday, I would have asked you to. Think about it, how big is a sheet of plywood?"

"Four feet by eight."

Dave's eyes are starting to twinkle again. "And did it ever occur to you that when your poor old uncle started planning to build a new home for Rita that he might have taken that into account?"

Mike stares at his uncle, contemplating his words. For a moment the pressing problems at work are forgotten. "You considered the standard size of a sheet of plywood when you planned the size of the addition—I mean, Rita's home?"

Dave nods his head gravely. “I hate running a saw any more than I absolutely have to, even more than I hate climbing ladders! Of *course* I took the precut size of the wood into account! It’s all about anticipating the work you’re creating for yourself. Just like Covey said 25 years ago, you begin with the end in mind. My goal wasn’t to make this hard on myself. I wanted the plywood to fit perfectly, with only a minimum of cuts with the saw.”

Dave’s eyes are shining with humor. “I believe we’ll find the joints fit a whole lot better using those nice, straight, factory-finished edges.”

In spite of his anxiety, Mike can’t help but laugh. “Dave, I’m out of my element here. I should have trusted you.”

The twinkle in Dave’s eyes fades to a sharp intensity, and he looks at Mike seriously. “I wonder if you’d trust me in areas that don’t have to do with building a home.”

Mike draws back in surprise. “What do you mean?”

“Mike, I don’t like to pry, but I could hear you talking on the phone while I was making lunch. It sounds like the person you were speaking with has you backed into a pretty tight corner.”

Mike carefully sets his sandwich down on the plate, untouched except for that first tentative bite. As much as he’d like to, he finds he still can’t look his uncle in the eye. “Yeah, I’m in a pretty bad spot.”

“Care to talk about it?” his uncle asks mildly.

Mike hesitates. "I don't like to burden other people with my problems." He pushes out a bitter chuckle. "And I've got a *lot* of problems! If I start talking, we might be sitting here all afternoon."

Dave leans back and looks up at the clear autumn sky. "I've got time if you've got the inclination to talk." He rests his hand lightly on Mike's shoulder for a moment. "Seriously, I don't want you to worry about getting the roof finished. There's more than enough time for that."

Mike shakes his head. "Oh, I don't know Uncle Dave. I don't think it will do any good to talk about it. It's just..."

Then suddenly, almost unbidden, the words pour out in a flash flood, "It's just that I'm worried that I'm in over my head. I've never felt this way before!"

Dave nods sympathetically and takes another bite of his sandwich, waiting.

"Everywhere I turn, I've got some new issue to deal with," Mike says harshly. He springs up off the stack of wood and begins pacing back and forth. "I've worked my butt off these last few years to make the business bigger, but it sure isn't better! I'm running around, putting out fires every day, and I've got no one to help me."

Mike's voice changes into a biting parody of an imaginary dim-witted manager. "I don't know what to do, Mike, so I called you," he wails. "I didn't want to make a move without talking to you first, Mike. Help me figure out how to make up my shift assignments, Mike.

Please call my customer for me, Mike."

He spins around, his eyes blazing. "You know why I'm never here with my family anymore? It's because my business demands *every* waking minute...and then some!" He snatches his cell phone off his belt and waggles it in front of Dave. "And when I *do* go home to be with my family, this thing never stops ringing. Never! Two o'clock in the morning! 'Mike, we've got an inventory control issue, and I don't know what to do!'"

Mike turns back toward the pond and cocks his arm, as if preparing to fling the phone out over the water. His voice is growing louder. "Do you know how many times I've wanted to just smash this thing against the wall?!" His arm arcs back even further. *It would feel so good to just give my cell phone a heave!*

"I remember what that felt like when I was growing my business." Dave's face pensive, his voice filled with reflection.

Somehow Dave's sympathetic tone causes Mike's frustration to boil over. "No, I don't think you *do* remember, Dave," he says sharply. "I've got just over 100 people looking to me—*me*—to make the right decisions, and I have to make *all* those decisions because none of my managers have the slightest idea how to manage! And if *that* wasn't enough, I've got customers calling all the time, wanting more, faster, better, cheaper, and what does my so-called sales force do? 'I'll have to talk to Mike,' they say. 'Mike, would you talk to so-and-so? He's unhappy because I made a promise that I *knew* I couldn't keep!' They're great at writing orders, but when it comes to actually *selling* something..."

"Had a few of those myself."

Mike's eyes flare wide. "Yeah? Well, did you have three different alphabet-soup federal agencies telling you who to hire and what to pay them and how to train them and laying down 30 different safety regulations for every step they take through the door?"

"As a matter of fact—"

"Aaaaah, never mind!" Mike pushes out a deep breath in an expression of impatience and disgust. "I'm sorry, Dave, but we're wasting our time here. I'm just venting and we need to get a roof up. We're two worlds apart."

Dave's eyes narrow as he considers his nephew before he quietly asks, "Why do you say that?"

"Because you don't have the slightest idea what I'm talking about." Mike is beyond thought. It's as if a haze has settled over his vision, making it impossible for him to see anything other than the vast array of problems that have been making his gut ache for the past two years. "You had your nice little lawn mowing business, and I'm trying to run a major distributorship."

"I'm beginning to think that you don't have the slightest idea what *you're* talking about."

There is a chill in Dave's voice that Mike has never heard before, forcing him to refocus. As quickly as his rage had flared, it disappears, leaving him feeling empty and utterly exhausted. He sinks slowly back onto the stack of plywood next to his uncle and puts his face in his hands, shaking his head slowly from side to side. "You're right, Uncle Dave. I thought for a while this morning that I might be looking at bankruptcy. I…I'm in a mess and I don't know what to do. I'm sure Dad would have known *exactly* how to handle this. I think I'm experiencing systemic failure verses systemic success."

He raises his gaze to look at Dave, expecting to see anger in his uncle's eyes. Instead there is that same loving kindness that he saw shortly after his father's death. "Dave…what I said just now…"

"Forget it." Dave's voice is kind, but there is a new note of authority Mike has never heard before. "We all say dumb stuff when we're frightened and angry."

Mike hangs his head again, looking down at the ground. "Dumb stuff," he echoes.

"Mike, I want to ask you a direct question and I want a direct answer."

Mike straightens up, his expression curious.

"Why do you believe that I wouldn't have any knowledge of what you're talking about?"

Mike winces. "I should never have said that."

"But you *believe* it," Dave says firmly. "Why?"

"Well..." Mike mentally searches for words that will not offend his uncle. "When I was a kid, I remember seeing you go off to work with a lawnmower in the back of your old pickup. Later on, when we were coming to visit here, you always had time for us. I...I guess I figured you must not have been too busy or overly stressed with work."

A smile tugs at the corners of Dave's mouth. "Which made you think that I didn't run a very challenging business?"

Mike nods wordlessly, guilt gnawing at him as he meets his uncle's gaze.

"So if I told you that Stillwell Landscape Services had 80 employees staffing three offices that would come as a surprise, huh?" Dave says drily.

Mike's eyes widen. "*Eighty* employees?"

"We had accounts with two federal office buildings, a military base, and a federal prison that we served year-round for twenty-five years, in addition to our other clients." Dave's lips thin slightly. "Now, I'll grant you that the feds have added regulation upon regulation in the last ten years or so, but I've had plenty of experience with OSHA and compliance issues and all the things you've just described. I dealt with it every day."

Mike cocks his head to the side slightly, eyeing his uncle in disbelief. "I had no idea."

"No, you didn't," Dave says, that businesslike tone is

back in his voice. "You had no idea because you never asked, and because you and Lee Anne were coming up here to get *away* from business, I never talked about mine. That wasn't because I didn't *have* challenges."

Mike is sitting stock still, staring at his uncle, cold realization washing over him. "And I've been sitting here, blathering on about my problems, actually thinking that you couldn't relate." He looks out over the pond and shakes his head again before looking back at Dave. "I'm afraid you have a nephew who isn't very observant."

To Mike's relief, Dave throws back his head and laughs. "I think there's a time in the life of almost every leader when he or she feels like it's 'me against the world,' and the world is winning! It's like you're caught inside this bubble, and no one else can see inside and relate to what you're feeling. You want more than anything else to get *out*, because the air inside that bubble is starting to get pretty thin, but you don't have the slightest idea how to do it. I was just like you, Mike. Ten years after I started my business, I was seriously considering declaring bankruptcy and going to work for somebody else."

Dave looks at Mike inquisitively. "Would you like to know who talked me out of it? My brother...your father."

"You talked to *Dad* about the problems with your business?"

"Sure! I knew he was having good success with the distributorship. I figured he knew principles that would help me with my issues." There is no mistaking the excitement in Dave's eyes now. "Maybe I can repay the favor by sharing some of those principles with you. Would you be interested in hearing my thoughts?"

"I'd be grateful to hear anything you would care to share," Mike says, still taken aback by how badly he misjudged his uncle.

"Great!" Dave takes one last swig of his ice tea and stands up. "Tell you what, I wanted to get the plywood and tar paper on before dark tonight. If we do that, we'll have the shingles done early tomorrow afternoon, and you can get home in plenty of time to enjoy dinner with your family. Let's get this work knocked out, then we can spend some good, solid time talking about systemic success over dinner tonight. OK?"

"Whatever you say, Uncle Dave," Mike says, surprised at the new hope he feels.

Cottage Takeaways

- Mike admits to himself that he does not know how to solve these problems.
- He is becoming aware that these are not unique problems to his business.
- As a result of focusing on top line growth, Mike inadvertently ignores the people side of the business.
- He admits there are processes to learn.

Chapter 4
Never "Just" Employees

The rest of the afternoon passes quickly. Mike is surprised at how smoothly the work goes. Uncle Dave has anticipated every step in the construction process, right down to laying out all the tools he and Mike will need and distributing them at the appropriate locations on the scaffolding surrounding the cottage. By five o'clock that evening, as the shadows are lengthening, all the plywood has been attached—requiring only minimal cuts, just as Dave had promised—and the tar paper is fastened in place.

As Mike and Dave are climbing down the scaffolding for the final time, Mike looks at Dave with undisguised admiration. "Dave, that was the most stress-free afternoon of work I've had in quite some time. Every task just flowed from one to the other. You had all the tools lined up and ready to go. I truly believed this morning we wouldn't get to this point until lunchtime tomorrow. At this rate, we might be *done* by lunchtime tomorrow!"

Dave winks at his nephew. "Like I said before, it's all

about taking a systemic approach. Now let me just get that grill fired up, then we'll pop a couple of cold beers and talk about how to get your business running just like this operation did today."

Mike looks at Dave with enthusiasm. "I've already picked up a few tips from today."

Dave has been rapidly wrapping a 50-foot extension cord around his arm, but he pauses. "Mike, let me ask you a question. Do you believe there are principles for business success that transcend industries?"

Mike's lips move into a wry smile. "You mean, principles that will work equally well in a landscaping company *and* a distributorship?"

Dave gives an emphatic nod, no trace of humor in his eyes. "That's *exactly* what I mean."

Dave slowly resumes wrapping up the extension cord, but his eyes are fixed on Mike's. "You said at lunch time that your father used to talk about taking a systemic approach in order to create systemic success, and that you wished you had listened more closely. Right?"

"That's *exactly* right," Mike says with feeling.

"Well, did your father ever mention that systemic success has three elements? Organizational success, organizational response, and individual response." Mike responds with a slow nod, searching to recall the context of his conversation with his father.

Dave continues, "As an organization achieves success, such as being profitable, creating shareholder value, delivering excellent customer service and so on, it creates opportunities for the organization to respond. Now, listen close, because this is critical." Dave gestures toward Mike, emphasizing his point. "Every organization responds to their success, or lack of success, every day. When I say respond I mean things like, investing in infrastructure, buying the right equipment, paying employees competitively, and investing in employee growth and development, things like that. The question is, is the response purposely planned, thus anticipating a desired outcome? Or, is the response left to chance? A response sets into motion a series of systemic events. Also keep in mind that no response is a response in itself."

Dave returns the wrapped extension cord to its proper place alongside the other neatly organized tools in the work cart.

"When a company experiences organizational success and creates a positive organizational response, it typically generates a positive individual response. This results in a higher level of engagement, greater discretionary effort, better safety performance, and more commitment and loyalty." Dave stares directly at Mike. "All the things I've heard you say were missing from your employees."

"As an employee, if the company is investing in me by providing the right leadership, proper equipment, training, and recognition, I would feel a higher sense of responsibility to do the best I can for the company. Mike, when a company responds, it creates an impression on its employees. This impression translates into a personal feeling that's displayed through their actions. One simple example of a negative feeling and how it manifests itself is through employee turnover. Do you follow me?"

Feeling like a kid again, soaking up his father's wisdom through his uncle, Mike nods his agreement.

Dave continues putting away the tools as he goes on. "Bottom line, Mike, when organizations respond positively, they get a positive individual response from their employees. *That* is how we create organizational success. We generate greater engagement, discretionary effort, and low turnover, which results in controlled cost, excellent customer service, higher profits, and improved shareholder value. All of which allows the organization to make *more* investments, creating an even *better* response. That's what your dad meant by 'systemic success.' Does that make sense?"

Mike has been listening so closely, he only now realizes that he hasn't been any help in the cleanup effort. "Yes, it does. When the organization succeeds, it can respond by making investments in infrastructure and people. That organizational response creates an individual response."

Dave's face splits into a bright smile. "Congratulations, Mike, you've got it!"

"The problem is, I'm not enjoying the organizational success that gets the ball rolling," Mike complains.

Even faced with Mike's negativity, Dave's smile does not waver. Instead, he claps Mike on the shoulder in support. "And *that's* what we're going to talk about over dinner."

The two men quickly finish cleaning up the jobsite, and within just a few minutes, they are seated on the front porch in the rocking chairs, sipping chilled mugs of beer. Dave sets a thick triangle of cheddar cheese on the table between them and pours some crackers into a bowl. "Dig in. It's gonna take a little while for the chicken to be ready."

Mike needs no further invitation. He cuts several generous slices of the tangy cheese for them both and pops a hunk in his mouth. "Mmm," he murmurs, chomping happily. "That tastes great!"

He takes a sip of beer and leans comfortably back in his chair.

Dave takes a long swallow from his mug. "Nothing like a cold beer after a hard day's work," he says with deep satisfaction, then he reaches for a notepad he brought out with the drinks and snacks. "I want to take some notes while we talk, OK?"

"Sure."

"So, I told you this afternoon that I can empathize—not just sympathize, but empathize—with how you're feeling about your business." Dave speaks slowly, choosing his words carefully. "There was a time when I was young and ambitious and I wanted to make a good living doing work that I loved. I worked a *ton* of hours—growing the business, making sales, hiring employees and people to manage them, trying to develop our internal infrastructure...and then one morning I woke up and realized I was like a hamster in a cage. I was running and running, but I wasn't making any progress. In fact, it seemed like the harder I ran, the worse things got. I was growing the business, but the problems, mistakes, and headaches were growing even more rapidly. The stress was starting to spill over into the way I was dealing with the staff and even the way I was behaving at home." Dave shakes his head and grimaces. "That is, when I actually *made* it home to do something other than sleep and shower and go back to work."

Mike has been watching his uncle talk, his eyes widening in surprise. He has always thought of Dave as one of the most self-assured, serene men he has ever known. It had never occurred to Mike that his uncle might have experienced a similar kind of tension. "Wow, Dave, I had no idea that you were—"

"Feeling like you do now?" Dave glances over at his nephew with a sad smile. "Mike, I think you may very well be handling it better than I did. My wife kept telling me to sell the business. She said no amount of money could make up for what the stress was doing to me."

Mike looks at his uncle with undisguised astonishment. "I just never had any inkling you were struggling like that!"

Dave waves a dismissive hand and gives Mike a kindly smile. "There's no reason you would have. This was all going on while you were still young, and besides, I didn't talk about it much. I think there are a great many leaders whose minds are constantly churning, problem-solving 24/7, but we don't say a word to the people around us. We feel like we have to internalize all this stress because if we display any vulnerability it will be perceived as weakness."

"I can certainly relate to that," Mike mumbles.

"I want to make sure I'm completely clear about the current state of your business." Dave's tone is more businesslike. "The first step is to feed back to you what I heard you saying this afternoon, and please feel free to correct me at any point where I'm mistaken or to add anything I've missed."

Mike is munching on another hunk of cheddar cheese. "Fire away," he says.

"Well," Dave begins, "from what you've told me, and from your half of the conversation I heard with your customer this morning, you wanted to grow the business from where it was when your dad died, and you've had some success in doing that, correct?"

"We've had *good* success with that," Mike replies. "We've doubled the size of our staff, and gross revenue is up more than 50%."

"That's impressive!" Dave says, his smile warm. "So you've done a very good job of beefing up the top line. But that hasn't translated to a corresponding increase on the bottom line?"

"Heavens, no!" Mike exclaims. "Last year, net income was only 8% higher than it was eight years ago."

"And you feel like you're doing 100% more work to bring in less than 10% more income?"

"You can say that again." Mike sighs. "More like 200% more work!"

"Can you tell me why that's happening?"

"I hate to sound like I'm pointing fingers away from myself," Mike replies. "I've failed to come up with the right answers, so the problem starts with me and me alone. With that said, I just don't feel like we have the quality of people we had when Dad was running the company. I honestly don't know what's changed. Obviously, we added the third shift, and turnover is always higher on an overnight shift, but it goes deeper than that. I feel like when my dad was running things, there was much greater loyalty. Yesterday we were struggling to get a delivery out and we had to call a temp service because no one would stay late or come in early."

Dave considers his nephew's words a moment before he speaks. "So you feel like your employees aren't really engaged with their work?"

"Not engaged?" Mike gives a snort of sarcastic laughter. "You should see them when the bell sounds at end-of-shift, Dave. They're lined right up at the time clock like somebody was giving away money!"

"Is money the problem? Are you losing people to companies who are offering more?" Dave asks.

"I guess there's some of that. I've always thought our compensation is competitive, but we just lost a really key person this week—our maintenance manager. He said it wasn't that he wanted more pay, but to work less hours. Yet he did get a sizeable raise from one of our competitors *and* they promised him less hours."

Dave jots some notes on the notepad before he asks, "How do you *know* your pay plan is competitive?"

Mike looks out over the pond for a long moment, as if the answer to Dave's question might suddenly pop up out of the water. When he finally replies, he does so with honesty. "When you ask me that, I guess I don't really know the answer."

Dave smiles and nods. "Fair enough. Any other people issues?"

Mike's eyes narrow with concentration. "Well, like I was telling you this morning, they just don't seem to like each other all that much. It's not that near-fights like the one we had this morning are common, but I don't sense that morale is very high. It seems to be every man for himself—and the mistakes they make! There are more and more all the time."

Dave makes another note, then looks at Mike closely. "What steps have you taken to address all this?"

Mike runs his fingers through his hair and sighs. "I've been so busy trying to hold everything together..."

"That's exactly how I felt," Dave says. "It's hard to paint the siding when you feel like the whole wall is falling down. How about the leaders in your organization? Do you discuss this together?"

"We talk about it all the time," Mike says irritably. "Much good that it does. I keep telling them they've got to tighten up and things keep getting worse, so I've tried tightening things up with *them*. Now they have to check with me before they make a major decision, but that means I'm stuck with a cell phone that rings all the time!"

"Hmm," Dave says thoughtfully. "Let me ask you this, Mike. What is your system for hiring? Have you taken steps to try to attract better quality staff and managers?"

"I sure have," Mike promptly responds. "We've announced a bonus for anybody who refers a friend or relative to come work with us. If the new hire completes his or her probationary period, the employee who referred them gets $100. I'm surprised we haven't had better success with that. We've only had two referrals in six months."

"Anything else?"

"Well, I post ads on job boards, and we're very specific about the skills we want. We try to hire people who don't require a whole lot of on-the-job training. I've told my VP of HR that she's got to get three references from all of our applicants and check all three."

"So you're looking to hire people who can step right in and do the job pretty much from the first day. Is that right?" Dave asks, scribbling another note on his pad of paper.

"Yes."

"OK, let's shift our focus. You're having some struggles with your employees. Are those struggles impacting your relationships with your customers?"

Mike groans. "That's one of the biggest changes since Dad died. I swear, new business used to practically come walking in the front door! I've beefed up our sales force and quadrupled our advertising budget. We *have* increased our account base, but with Dad, they were like his friends. Today, most of our customers are unhappy! It seems like much more of an adversarial relationship. It's a fight to get new customers and an even bigger fight to keep them."

"Mike, I want to ask you one more question, and I really appreciate how forthcoming you've been."

"Ask me anything you want," Mike says, relieved to finally be getting some of this off his chest.

"What are you trying to achieve?"

"I just want things to run more smoothly," Mike replies, without even having to pause and think about his answer.

Dave grins. "Your father asked me that same question, and I said exactly the same thing! Tell me a little more. Is that all you want? Just smooth sailing?"

Mike hesitates, thinking over Dave's question. He truly wants to be honest with his uncle.

"When I was in college," he finally says, "Dad said something to me about having systems in place that took care of 50 families. They were never just 'employees' to him, Dave. I'm sure you know that. He saw *people*, and he valued them. He knew their names, their spouses' names, their kids' names. He cared about their success. He'd get really excited when one of our employees bought a new home or had a kid who graduated from college. I remember one time he spent several minutes talking to a woman who was going to thrift stores to buy furnishings for her family's new home, their first one. He took such joy in it! For Dad, it was almost like he felt he was a part of that."

"Now, that's interesting. So your picture of success has more to it. Your dad talked to me about that very thing." Dave leans closer to Mike, his voice soft with recollection. "He said people are trying so hard, often having to get by on very little, and yet they were still giving him their day and giving him their best. He said he felt obligated to help them be successful. He *wanted* them to be successful."

"Yes, that was Dad." Mike is suddenly overcome with realization. "Dave, I'm afraid my employees don't see me as that kind of person." Then, almost as if he is speaking to himself, Mike murmurs, "You know what?

I am that person, but I haven't done a good job of showing it. I've been so focused on sales and growing the business and the problems that go with all that..."

Mike's voice trails off. Suddenly he shakes his head. "How can my employees *think* I care about them as people when I don't *show* them that I care?"

Mike is deep in thought, looking down at the wooden planks on the front porch, so he does not see the bright light of excitement shining in his uncle's eyes.

"Mike, I want you to think carefully," Dave says. "Do you want to run a business in which your employees are cared about and cared for, so in return they will care about and care for your customers? Is that what you want?"

Mike looks up at his uncle. "I want that more than anything in the world," he says emphatically. "I don't *want* to make more money if it means we're going to have a reputation for this kind of dysfunction. I want to have a good reputation with my customers *and* my employees. I want my employees to look at me the way they looked at my dad. I want them to trust me and respect me for all the *right* reasons—because I genuinely care about them and I'm running a really good business that they can be proud of."

Dave slaps his knee and grins with sheer delight. "I believe I can help you accomplish that. I'm sure of it! Now, let's go get that chicken off the grill and we'll go inside and get to work on engineering a process that will make that happen."

Cottage Takeaways

- Mike learns the interdependent relationship of organizational success, organizational response, and individual response. Organizational success is the outcome of individual response. Individual response is the outcome of organizational response.
- Organizational response creates an impression on its employees. This impression translates into personal feelings that are displayed through their actions (attendance, turnover, commitment to success, safety, and quality).
- Organizations respond every day to their success or lack of success. The goal is to manage organizational response to achieve higher levels of engagement and discretionary effort. Through higher levels of engagement and discretionary effort, companies achieve controlled cost, higher profits, improved shareholder value, and customer retention.

Chapter Five
"Curveballs"

"Mike, from what you've described to me, the problems you're facing are systemic in nature," Dave says.

The two men are seated inside the cottage now after devouring a delicious meal of barbequed chicken, corn, a fresh salad, and a hot loaf of French bread. They quickly cleared the dining room table and Dave produced a pot of fresh, steaming coffee and two cups.

Mike reaches for the coffee pot and fills both of their cups. "Systemic problems?"

Dave takes a sip of the hot coffee and nods with satisfaction. "Business leaders must always be thinking systemically. We're always trying to manage toward systemic success and away from systemic failure, right? The only problem is our work inevitably throws us curveballs—events that we didn't anticipate. Those curveballs come at us from many different directions, sometimes from our own employees, and every one of these curveballs can impact our business."

"Give me an example." Mike asks.

"A curveball is an unexpected event. On the surface it may seem small and insignificant, but a curveball often requires an organizational response. Like we discussed earlier, this can start a chain of systemic events—say, an employee who has attendance issues. His poor attendance leads to overtime for people who don't really want to work late. In turn, the organization responds by requiring overtime of workers who are tired and not particularly engaged. This can lead to quality issues, because we don't have the right people, doing the right jobs, at the right time."

Dave pauses to take another sip of coffee. "Those quality issues lead to poor production and inferior service, and *that* leads to unhappy accounts, which leads to *losing* accounts, which affects profitability to the point where you can't make the type of investment you need to make to run the business successfully. Remember, organizational success creates organization response (investments), which leads to individual response."

Dave leans back in his chair and looks at Mike. "Does any of that sound familiar?"

Mike's eyes widen. "Familiar? It sounds *exactly* like what I'm dealing with every day!"

Dave nods, his expression serious. "I was facing the same problems and that hypothetical example illustrates the impact on the entire business that comes from just one curveball: an employee who fails to show up to work. I'm sure you and I could come up with a list of dozens of other curveballs. Our tardy worker is an example of the systemic failure we're trying to manage away from. The question is, how do we go about managing toward systemic success?"

Mike can't help but grin. "That's what I was hoping you were about to tell me."

"The theory for business success that your dad showed me is simply complicated." Dave reaches for his notepad, returning Mike's grin. "It's very simple, but sometimes the 'simple' things aren't that easy! They appear to be easy in concept, but they can be complicated in deployment because many business leaders forget to think in terms of an integrated system."

Mike remembers pondering the phrase "simply complicated" in the car yesterday afternoon. "You know, Dave, that was one of dad's favorite phrases for conversations like this."

Dave laughs. "Yes, I've heard it many times!" He writes a few words on the notepad before he swings it around for Mike to see. "Here's the formula for business success: people, process, and product."

Mike repeats the three words slowly: "People... Process...Product."

All Businesses are Centered around 3 Things...

My People Systems need Help!

PEOPLE

PROCESS

PRODUCT

"That's it," Dave says with approval. "From everything you've told me, Mike, you don't have a product problem; you already have a good product. The product will take care of itself, *if* you have the right people operating within the right processes. Do you remember when I visited your company just over a year ago?"

Mike nods.

"You took me back to the warehouse and showed me how you're utilizing technology to improve your inventory processes. You've done a good job there! I know you're using the right processes and you've invested wisely in the right technology. Given the difficulties you've described in providing superior service to your customers, it may be that your people processes need attention."

"Yes, I can see that," Mike says thoughtfully. "I made significant capital investments in buildings, equipment, and technology that I thought would make us successful. Investments, I figured, would help my people succeed. In my mind, we *should* be doing much better."

"So let's talk about how to help your people succeed." Dave is writing on the notepad again. "I want to focus on a systemic approach to hiring, developing, and retaining the best people."

"So the problem with my business is my *employees*?" Mike asks, his brow furrowed with uncertainty.

Dave chuckles at his nephew's reaction. "No, they're not the problem. They are the key to your ongoing success, *if* you develop a sustainable system to hire, develop, and retain the best employees for your business."

"I'm missing something," Mike says. "We've tried to get referrals for good employees, and we've had very little success."

"No, no, no. Offering a finder's fee for referring a hire isn't exactly the type of 'system' I'm referring to, Mike," Dave says evenly. "It's only one small component of the system. Let's talk about that system for a minute."

"It starts with how you fill open positions and how that has evolved over time. Back when your dad and I were kids, an employer would simply put a 'Help Wanted' sign in front of the building and place an ad in the local newspaper. Those classified ads are rapidly becoming a thing of the past, just as the 'Help Wanted' signs disappeared from the front of the building."

"Then the internet began to flourish, and this new technology allowed you to utilize job boards, like Monster and Career Builder. You'd post an ad and people sitting at home could respond electronically—that is, if they were actively looking for a job to start with. Well, today even these job boards are being replaced by candidate sourcing. Are you familiar with the term?"

"Somewhat. Our HR manager has mentioned it to me before." He lifts his shoulders in a half-hearted shrug. "I've just been so busy, I haven't really looked into it more."

"That's okay," Dave says. "There are plenty of business leaders who are just coming to understand the power of candidate sourcing. Here's how it works. You told me you lost your maintenance manager this week, so you'll be searching for a replacement. If you put an ad on a job board, you're hoping the right person with the required skills is looking at that job board at the very same time you post the opening."

Dave pauses to make sure Mike is following.

At Mike's nod, Dave continues. "So there's an 'x' and 'y' axis you're trying to intersect. A chance that you have that job opening and the chance that the best person to fill that opening is looking for a position at the same time. If those events don't intersect perfectly, you end up with compromise on both sides. You, the employer, compromise by taking the best person available at that time. The person you hire may also be compromising—Stillwell Distributors has the best job available at the moment, but not necessarily the position or even the work environment the person is really looking for. When you use the job boards you usually end up with both sides compromising."

"Kind of like winning the lottery," Mike says, the light of understanding shining in his eyes. "You need to buy the winning ticket the same week that those winning numbers are drawn."

"That's exactly right!" Dave responds with approval. "Now, with candidate sourcing, what happens is you utilize a sourcer or team of sourcers, whose job it is to go out and find the very best candidates—much like a recruiter does—but these sourcers use the internet, databases, networks, and other industry technology to find the people who match your job criteria, whether they're currently looking for a job or not. It's a more proactive, research-oriented approach to finding talent. So you activate this team of sourcers, and while you go on to attend to your business, they're looking for the very best job applicants. In a short period of time, you have a pool of potential new hires who don't even know you're looking for a new maintenance manager."

"You then turn that list over to your best internal recruiter who can call those individuals and say, 'I'd like to tell you about an opportunity you may be interested in,' much like a headhunter does. You already know that this list of people matches your qualifications. Now you can start the interviewing process and using your assessment tools to help you identify the right person or people to whom you're ready to make an offer."

Mike is looking at his uncle quizzically. "Were you using this candidate sourcing for *your* business?"

Dave laughs. "Of course not! It wasn't available. I've run the entire gamut of hiring practices. When I started my business, I used to tape 'Now Hiring' signs to the doors on my pickup. By the time I retired, I was posting on job boards, but I knew that technology was changing and the process for recruiting people was evolving rapidly. I've always been fascinated with how businesses attract, develop, and retain the best people. The things I read today about technology and the advancements in recruiting amaze me! No one is leaving it to chance anymore. These integrated systems that utilize the latest technology for recruiting talent go way beyond job boards."

"There are a great many companies who still leave it to chance. They'll say, 'Well, I posted it on a job board...' and hope for the best." Dave laughs. "But we know hope is not a strategy. Other companies are actively searching to find *exactly* the right people. They're not trying to win the lottery, like you said. Those companies have a much greater opportunity for success. This candidate sourcing used to happen only with executive searches conducted by recruiters, but in recent years it has been used to fill a broad range of jobs, even semi-skilled positions. That happens all the time now. Today, in so many more cases than in the past, employers are able to create the perfect intersection without having to compromise."

"I've read about how this sourcing has been used to hire people for technical skills," Mike says, his expression showing his surprise. "But I had no idea companies have been using it so broadly!"

Dave leans toward Mike, excited to be sharing this knowledge with him. "You always want to be leading edge when it comes to recruiting. You want to utilize the best processes for hiring the best people. *Never* leave it to chance. Never cut yourself short in this area. Before you do anything else, you want to attract and hire the best people."

Mike nods firmly, then grins as he says, "Simply complicated!"

Dave smiles back in response. "That's still just one aspect of the system, though. We've talked about utilizing the latest processes and technology; now let me show you how to plug that into a system that your dad taught me years ago."

As Dave is sketching on the notepad Mike goes into the kitchen and pours two fresh cups of coffee. When he returns, he notices Dave has finished sketching.

Dave swings the notepad around, saying, "Take a look at this."

Mike reads:

Mike looks at the words carefully, and then glances up at his uncle, his brow furrowed. "I'm going to need a little help with this."

Dave chuckles. “Don’t worry, we’ll go through these in turn, but before we do that, let’s talk about why it’s important to put such a system in place.”

“OK,” Mike willingly agrees. “I’m all ears.”

“Thirty years ago your dad told me if I didn’t listen to anything else he said, I should remember this—and I have! It became the distribution center of every decision I made from that point forward. You probably heard him say these things before, but *this* is the foundation for everything else I’m going to tell you tonight.”

Mike feels his anticipation growing at Dave’s build up. “Tell me!” he says eagerly.

“The most important partner any company has is its employees. They create the brand and live in its image. Employees are either a company’s greatest advocate or its worst enemy. When employees are valued, cared for, developed, and treated with respect, a company will flourish. When they’re treated as if they’re no more important than any other material resource, the company will never achieve its highest potential.”

“You’re right,” Mike agrees, his eyes squinting as he thoughtfully recalls the past. “I *do* remember Dad saying all of that, although maybe not altogether like you just did. He used to say that if your people shine, the company will shine and your customers will notice.”

“Exactly.” Dave nods emphatically. “Your employees *are* your brand! Your brand is not your unique selling proposition. Your brand isn’t what your marketing materials say it is. It isn't even the promises your sales force makes. All of those can be duplicated by your competition. There are only two things that truly set companies apart. The first is your employees and how your employees perform. A second possible differentiator is a technology that you have developed and hold a patent on that nobody else has. But then again, your employees are the ones who develop, utilize, and maintain that specialized technology, so it really comes right back to the employees. They are your brand, Mike. Everything else can be copied or imitated, but your brand identity is firmly established in the mind of your community and your customers by the interactions they have with your employees."

"I understand," Mike agrees. "Our employees are the face of our business."

"It's even more far-reaching than that," Dave continues. "Your brand is created by the interactions that *each* of your stakeholders have with all your employees. I used to think it was just the so-called 'front line' people who established the brand, the people who had the face-to-face with the paying customers. But I wasn't thinking systemically, so I was missing a big piece of the picture."

"The drivers who come to your distribution center to pick up or drop off merchandise, we might not think of them as 'customers,' but they interact with members of your staff, and then they go off to their next stops, and then they go home. Those drivers often talk about the experience they had at your distribution center, particularly if it's a very positive experience...and especially if it's a very negative one. Your employees create the brand for those drivers, and those drivers share your brand with the people they interact with as well. That's true for the vendors and service personnel who come in and out of your organization. Their interactions with your staff create your brand image for those visitors. In many cases, the employees they interact with weren't necessarily hired for their people skills, but for other reasons. Yet, they inevitably create the brand for dozens of people."

"You mentioned you have government contracts, so from time to time, you have compliance officers from the government come to visit with you. They interact with different members of your team, and they too will speak to others of their experience at Stillwell Distributors." Dave pauses, looking at Mike to make sure he's following along. "Do you see where I'm going with this?"

Mike nods thoughtfully. "There's a systemic effect. Our employees are creating a word-of-mouth advertising that may or may not be what I'd like."

"That's right," Dave says. "Let's say a driver has a bad experience on your loading dock with an employee who is rude or careless—"

"Or both," Mike mutters.

"Yep, or both." Dave chuckles. "That driver goes off to his next stop, and the people there treat him and his merchandise with care. He didn't necessarily leave your facility with the intent of badmouthing your company, but as his truck is being loaded, he tells the people at this stop how badly it went for him at Stillwell Distributors. Then one or two of the people who were part of that conversation tell somebody *else*, and—"

"And it doesn't matter what our unique selling proposition is," Mike interrupts wryly. "We've established our brand in a way that we never wanted or intended."

"I'm afraid so." Dave frowns, his face marking his unhappiness. "On the other hand, there are the people you *do* hire and pay largely for the way they interact with your customers. A sales rep feels pressured to meet and exceed her sales quotas, so she promises turnaround times that are unrealistic. Or maybe someone in customer service feels underpaid or unappreciated; she takes an inbound phone call and speaks brusquely to a customer. Those two employees have established your brand in ways that you didn't want also."

"Oh, Dave," Mike says on a sigh, "it sounds like you've been talking to some of our customers. I've fielded complaint calls about all of the things you've mentioned so far."

"There are also the things you'll *never* get a call about, Mike," Dave continues grimly. "A husband goes home and tells his wife and kids over dinner how much he hates his job, because his boss only talks to him about output and quotas. The next day his wife goes to *her* job and tells her friends that Stillwell Distributors doesn't care about its people."

"A wife comes home and vents to her husband about

her boss using inappropriate language in front of her colleagues. Thursday night the husband goes to his bowling league, and over beers after the game he tells his buddies that Stillwell Distributors hires idiots for managers. One of the men on his team is a purchasing agent for a company that one of your sales reps is trying to close for a distribution contract. All of a sudden that buyer no longer has time to talk to your rep. Your brand is set in his mind. Maybe he goes to lunch the following week with one of his peers who is looking to change distributors. The name of your company comes up, and the bowling league man tells his friend that he's heard Stillwell Distributors is poorly managed. That's the kind of unintentional advertising that *no* company needs!"

Mike grimaces and shakes his head. "That's probably a pretty accurate description of what a great many people believe about us."

"Are you sure? Do you know what people believe about you?"

Mike sighs with resignation. "I talked to a customer just this morning who told me we've lost our way."

"I didn't mean your customers," Dave persists. "I mean, do you know what your employees are thinking and feeling? Do you know what your employees say about your brand?"

Mike looks at Dave blankly. "I...no, I don't. Based on the lack of loyalty, I guess they don't think too much of it."

"Finding out your employees' opinions about your workplace might be one of the most important things you can do right now, Mike."

I pay them to do a job! Mike thinks angrily. *Their "opinion" should be that they're responsible to do a good job!* He sits silently, brooding. *But what Dave says about "unintentional advertising" is right on the money. And it's true that I don't have the slightest idea what our employees think or feel. I always figured our managers were keeping their ears open for that sort of thing.*

Mike looks up at his uncle plaintively. "Dave, I don't want to seem argumentative, but it just seems to me that I need to concentrate on fixing our customer service issues. If we're operating efficiently, our brand image will take care of itself."

Dave leans closer to his nephew. His voice is low and intense. "Of course you're *right* to be concerned about your customers' satisfaction, but I must stress to you that the relationship with your customers is a systemic result of the relationship you have with your employees. Mike, you have to recognize this and accept it as truth if we're going to advance from here: Your employees *are* your brand. Your brand lives through them and that brand is reflected in their work. That reflection is then cast upon your customers, and those customers will decide to do business with you—or *not*—as a direct result of that reflection."

"Yes, I see that." Mike shakes his head frowning as he takes another sip of coffee. "But, it's frustrating because it is their *job* to treat our customers well!"

Dave's expression fills with chagrin. "You know, when your dad first started talking to me about these concepts, I had a lot of doubts about what he was saying, just like you probably do right now. Then your father asked me the same question that I'm going to ask you; was I was frustrated enough with the way my business was operating to try something new?" Dave chuckles, "Believe me, I definitely was!"

Dave's face grows serious again, and he waits silently, staring at his nephew with an unspoken question: *How frustrated are you, Mike?*

After a moment, Mike answers softly, "I am *really* frustrated. You keep talking; I'm ready to try something new."

Cottage Takeaways

- Curveballs are unexpected events or events that are out of our control, such as changes in legislation, new development in technology, unexpected absences, etc.
- Curveballs typically require an organizational response. This response must be managed in order to get the desired individual response.
- The formula for business success centers around three principles: people, process, product. Mike's problem is with his people.
- His lack of integrated people systems is causing him systemic failures with his process and product.
- Mike develops a deeper understanding of the following statement: "The most important partner any company has is its employees. They create the brand and live in its image. Employees are either a company's greatest advocate or its worst enemy. When employees are valued, cared for, developed, and treated with respect, a company will flourish. When they are treated as if they are no more important than any other material resource, the company will never achieve its highest potential."
- Business leaders must always be thinking systemically. For example, customer relationships can be a systemic result of the relationship you have with your employees.

Chapter Six

"I Do, I Am, I've Done, I Know"

As the coffee pot runs dry, Dave invites Mike to get some fresh air on the front porch. They sit in two rockers separated by a small table with a twisted nail puzzle on it. Mike recognizes it and remembers trying to solve the puzzle as a kid. He picks it up and fumbles with it for a moment before Dave gently takes it from his hands and with a simple twist, separates the two nails. He looks over at Mike and says with a smile—"Simply Complicated."

"Now let's talk about what 'something new' will look like." Dave taps the diagram on his pad. "A big part of what your dad taught me centered around a system for *people*—a system that will advance your brand in the most positive way possible. There are three elements to that system: **Hire to your success profile**, **develop for performance and succession**, and **retain the best people with engagement**. I want to take you through these, one-by-one."

"So we start with hiring to a success profile. When I

asked about how you hire earlier, it sounded like you look for people with the right skill sets. Is that correct?"

"Absolutely," Mike's tone suggests that there is no other way to hire.

"So you try to hire the most skilled employees?"

"Of *course* we hire for skills," Mike says with a touch of impatience. "We don't want to spend a whole lot of time training people and putting up with their mistakes. I just had a guy today who knocked over a palette and damaged some goods. That's what happens when you put rookies in place."

"Hmm," Dave pensively says. "But you say your people aren't loyal."

"Yes, but what's that got to do with—"

"And even the experienced people you hire make mistakes?"

"Well...yes. They make a *lot* of mistakes," Mike admits. "You mentioned curveballs before. New hires throw me a *lot* of curveballs. We hire somebody who looks great, but they turn out to be indifferent workers. We hire somebody else who has all the skills and all the initiative you could ever want, but they leave not long after we hire them."

Dave nods. "What is the most important characteristic your employees must possess?"

"I don't know if I can pinpoint any one thing," Mike says slowly. He thinks for a moment before he continues. "I want someone who cares about doing the job right as much as I do. Give me someone who has passion." Suddenly his words start to come with more intensity. "Give me someone who has integrity and takes pride in their work, someone who is honest, loyal, and respectful. I want people who are willing to learn and who know how to treat the customer like I would treat them."

Dave has been jotting notes while Mike has been speaking. He pauses for a moment, staring down at his notepad.

"Mike," he says thoughtfully, "I've never driven a fork-lift before. I've operated other equipment, but I've never even sat on a fork truck. How long would it take you to train me to operate one?"

"I can train anyone with good motor skills to operate the lift safely and efficiently. Somebody like you, with a good attitude and good mechanical aptitude...it wouldn't take any time at all. Shoot," Mike says with a grin, "I'd do anything to have an employee like you, Uncle Dave."

Dave does not return his smile. "But your company would never interview me for the position," he says softly. "I wouldn't make it through your screening process because I don't have fork truck experience."

Mike opens his mouth to reply, but no words come out.

Dave looks back down at the notepad, tapping it with his pen. "I asked you to name the most important characteristic an employee at Stillwell Distributors could possess, and you didn't say one thing about their skill sets; it was all about their mind set. You didn't say you wanted someone who was the best fork truck operator or the best customer service rep. You talked about character."

Dave gives his nephew a gentle smile. "You see where I'm going with this, don't you? You're setting out to hire people with good fork truck skills, but what you really want are people with good character traits. You say you'd love to have an employee like me, but you're not currently looking to hire employees like me."

Mike's eyes are widening with surprise and new understanding. "That thought simply never occurred to me before!"

Dave chuckles. "Don't feel bad, Mike. I was making the same mistake in my company. I was trying to hire people who had the right skills for my landscaping business, but skill wasn't solving our customer service issues."

"More and more major companies are starting to understand this. Just this week a friend e-mailed me an article about Southwest Airlines. I don't know how often you fly, but you may have heard how Southwest consistently ranks as one of the top US Airlines in terms of numbers of passengers and profitability. The company is legendary for their upbeat culture. Clearly, they're doing something right when it comes to hiring the right people! What was so interesting about this article is that Southwest examines three primary factors when evaluating potential new hires, and *none* of those three factors had to do with skills. They all were about attitude."

Mike gazes at his uncle closely, connecting the dots Dave has laid out for him. "That reminds me of Jim Collins' *Good to Great* book, which was such a big best-seller. One of Collins' maxims was that you must get the right people on the bus." Mike pauses and nods his head in dawning realization. "He didn't say to get the right skill sets on the bus."

"Exactly right," Dave says with approval. "I saw a feature on the news a few years back about Four Seasons Hotels, considered to be one of the top luxury hotels in the world. They talked about the great care they take in selecting the right people. One of their managers said something like, 'I can't train people to care; I *can* teach them to be competent.' Four Seasons looks to hire good *people;* then they train them to be good hotel employees. Companies like Southwest and Four Seasons hire for attitude and cultural fit and then develop the professional skills, rather than hiring for skills and hoping the employee will fit their culture."

"Dave, I have to admit that's never been a part of my hiring philosophy. It's funny that Dad and I never talked about that."

"Not so funny, really. I'm sure he was planning to, but he just never got the chance."

"Yeah," Mike says softly.

It's now almost seven o'clock and the sun is setting,

so Dave gets up and turns on the front porch lights. "OK, let's start a to-do list for you." Dave pulls a clean sheet of paper off the notepad. "It will benefit you tremendously to document what a successful employee looks like. You and your leaders should then sit down together and discuss the attributes you're looking for to match the culture you want."

"Okay..." Mike says slowly. "I'm not quite sure I understand."

Dave is already writing quickly and confidently on the notepad, but he pauses to grin at Mike's discomfort. "Never fear, Mike. Remember when you thought that putting the roof on Aunt Rita's new home was way too much for you and me to do in a weekend?"

"Ouch!" Mike groans. "And you'd been so gracious not to remind me about that."

Dave's hearty laugh fills the porch. "Do you remember what I said was going to make the job manageable? Two phrases..."

"I believe it was 'a systemic approach for systemic success,' right?"

"Excellent!" Dave's face lights up and he is clearly pleased. "So let me introduce you to a system that will allow you to create a **success profile** for potential new hires at Stillwell Distributors. Give me just a moment here."

Mike watches with interest as his uncle completes the following diagram on the notepad.

LEADERSHIP Success Profile

Capabilities	Experience
• Lead change / Create Engagement • Relationships & Partnerships • Develop & Deploy a Vision • Achieve Through People • Drive Performance What I Do	• Internal & External Organization • Functions Worked • Accountability & Delivery What I've Done
Personal Attributes	**Knowledge**
Who I Am • Emotional Intelligence • Professional Disposition • Drive to Achieve • Ownership / Integrity	What I Know • Your Organization • Your Competitors • Key Business Processes • The world, outside of Your Business

"Here's the system." Dave clears the chess pieces and sets the notepad in front of Mike. "You can use these four quadrants for any organization. They transcend companies and industries, and you'll always use the same four quadrants no matter what: **Capabilities, Experience, Personal Attributes**, and **Knowledge**. On the diagram these are simply defined as **'What I Do,' 'What I've Done,' 'Who I Am,'** and **'What I Know.'"**

Mike's eyes narrow as he studies the diagram. "When you say these things, I vaguely remember hearing Dad say something about 'hiring to a success profile' on more than one occasion. I'm afraid I didn't pay a whole lot of attention."

Dave claps Mike on the shoulder in support. "Just like every other young man who turns 16 and suddenly believes he knows more about everything in life than his father does!"

Mike smiles ruefully, but suddenly his face shadows as he feels a deep sense of sadness. Dave's quip has come uncomfortably close to accurately describing Mike's attitude in high school and college.

Dave can see Mike's discomfort, and he says kindly, "But that's really okay, Mike, because the success profile your father used probably won't be the same profile you will use today since you've grown the business. You've made a lot of changes, many of them very *good* changes, but the elements of the profile I'm about to show you—these four quadrants on the diagram—remain constant over time and they apply to all endeavors. That's what makes this concept universally successful. It worked for me in landscaping and for your father in distribution."

For the first time in a long while, Mike starts to feel optimistic. He realizes it's within his ability to make the changes necessary to positively impact his company's performance.

"I'm eager to learn it, Dave," Mike says warmly.

Dave gives Mike an encouraging smile. "Let's start in the upper-right quadrant. **Experience,** of course, is **'What I've Done.'"** Dave looks up at Mike inquisitively. "Your hiring focus had been primarily on this quadrant, correct? You're focused primarily on previous experience?"

Mike nods a ready affirmative, still studying Dave's document.

"Well, you're certainly not alone. A lot of companies hire to experience—and please don't interpret me saying you should *ignore* someone's experience. What I *am* saying is that experience is only one quarter of a solid success profile."

Mike nods and his gaze locks on Dave. "By looking primarily at experience, I've been missing the complete package."

"That's right." Dave smiles with approval. "Let's move down to the lower-right-hand quadrant—**Knowledge** is **'What I Know.'** This is usually the second quadrant that people hire to. For a long time, I was one of those people. Employers look at an applicant and think, 'OK, he or she has *done* this—they have the experience I'm looking for—and in addition to that, they *know* about our industry, so that's a plus. If their references check out and they pass the drug test, I'll hire them.'"

"But here's what I was missing, Mike: It's a fact that people are often successful because of what they do and who they are. That's their **Capabilities** and **Personal Attributes**, and all too often we completely neglect to define what we're looking for in these areas, much less hire for them."

The doubt and confusion have vanished from Mike's eyes, and he is looking keenly at his uncle now. "Keep going, Dave. Tell me more about these quadrants."

Dave nods, grinning at Mike. He hasn't missed the change in his nephew's demeanor, and is eager to teach these principles that so effectively transformed his own business. "When I sketched out this particular success profile, I was thinking in terms of an individual contributor to your company, like an entry-level warehouse worker, a fork truck driver, or a maintenance specialist. They don't manage other people. They work as part of a team, and all contribute as individuals, but they're not supervisors, managers, or leaders."

"Again, Mike, I don't want to belabor the point, but this is a *system* of management, so you and your team should work together and define just what each of these four quadrants looks like in your organization. Then you would create a second success profile for the men and women you're looking to hire at the supervisory or management level. That profile will still have the same four quadrants, but the descriptions may be different. At some point, you'll also want to create a success profile for the director level or a vice president-executive level."

"So we use the same four quadrants, whether it's an individual contributor, manager, or an executive. Capabilities, Experience, Knowledge, and Personal Attributes," Mike says, tapping each quadrant in turn. "But the descriptions for each quadrant may differ according to the level you're talking about."

"Correct," Dave says. "So now let's swing back to the upper-left corner of the success profile and look at **Capabilities**, that is, **'What I Do.'** Now, when you and I are looking at an individual contributor—someone who does not direct others—we might very well wonder, 'How does an individual contributor *lead change* or *create engagement*?' There was a time when I would have said, 'They don't! Individual contributors don't lead change.' It was your dad who told me emphatically, 'They most certainly *do*!'"

Mike looks curiously at his uncle. "How so? I always thought it was the role of an organization's senior leaders to create change."

"That's what I thought, too!" Dave exclaims. "And please don't misunderstand me. The success profile *must* be supported by leadership behavior. That means *you*, Mike. You have to model *all* the descriptions there, not just leading change. That's a really important part of the equation. It's not enough to put the profile in place; you've got to be a living model of the qualities described in the profile."

"But think about this, individual contributors lead by their attitude and their actions. When you initiate change at Stillwell Distributors, how each individual contributor accepts that change—their willingness to support it, what they say about it to their coworkers, and how they comply with it—is all part of leading change."

"Mike, you may very well have people who work for your company who sit in the break room complaining about the things they don't like at work. They're leading change in that moment! Maybe they're griping about something their shift manager just introduced to the entire team in the morning meeting. They're setting an example and exercising leadership in that moment, no matter what their job title is. As an example, a co-worker says, 'Look, guys, I don't have this new initiative all figured out either, but we've got to be nimble, we must be able to adapt and learn new things. I'm going to give it my best shot.' That person is leading change in a completely different direction from the person who's sitting there grumbling, 'I'm not gonna do that!' Your individual contributors are leading change, Mike, one way or another. The question is, are they going to lead in the way you *want* your employees to be led?"

Mike thrums his fingers on the table as he lets Dave's words sink in, a new understanding dawning within him. "People lead by example. They can either lead others to do a good job and work hard alongside them... or to gossip and complain. They lead by coming in ten minutes early, so that they're actually starting work on time, rather than coming in five minutes late and taking an additional ten minutes to pour their coffee and get squared away. They can lead people to rally together and adopt the attitude of 'Let's work hard and do the job right,' or they may lead people to be lackadaisical and take shortcuts. That lackadaisical attitude is *killing* us right now!"

"So when you sit down with your leadership team, Mike, you look at this subject of *Leading Change*—" Dave taps the notepad with a finger to emphasize his point, "—and ask each other this question: **'What are the qualities that are most important for an individual contributor's success in our organization?'** When you've identified those qualities and written them down, that's what you look for during your hiring process."

"I can think of a number of those qualities myself," Mike says, jotting some notes on his pad.

"I'm sure you can," Dave agrees. "And now we come to the last quadrant—one that is often overlooked, but is so vitally important—the lower-left quadrant, **Personal Attributes.** This refers to **'Who I Am.'** Mike, when I asked you to name what the most important characteristic an employee at Stillwell Distributors should possess, you didn't say anything about 'Can drive a fork truck' or 'Knows the road to the sale.' Instead, you talked about qualities like passion, integrity, taking pride in a job well done, loyalty, and respect. These are all things that fall into that 'Who I Am' quadrant. So, clearly, that quadrant is hugely important to you."

Mike's shoulders slump. "Except we haven't been *hiring* for those qualities. We've never even discussed it."

"In fact," Dave continues, "right now you have people who may or may not meet the success profile themselves recommending to you whom you should hire next. Without realizing it, your hiring process—if you really want to call it a 'process'—is actually perpetuating your people problem."

Mike winces and nods his acknowledgment of this truth.

"It's not just you, Mike. There are many business leaders who hire exactly the same way that you've been. When I sold my company ten years ago, I had a long talk with the buyers about this very concept. I asked them, 'What is the single most important characteristic for success in your business?' And just like you, they couldn't pinpoint any one thing. They said, 'We want someone who can pass the drug test, who shows up on time, who doesn't start trouble in the workplace, and who's willing to learn the jobs that we need done. We want people who are eager to learn and contribute.' They never said *one word* about, 'wanting someone who can operate the equipment.' Why? Because they can teach the new hire how to run the mowers, just like you can teach me to drive a fork truck."

"What they wanted, first and foremost, were people who would show up to work hard every day and work cheerfully and professionally. However, their interview process focused only on experience and skills. They had never created a profile that describes what success looks like and then consciously worked to identify the men and women who fit that description and hire them."

Mike stares intently at Dave's "Success Profile" document. "This could make a *huge* difference in the character and quality of our operation."

Dave nods supportively. "And this success profile doesn't work just for hiring, Mike. You also fold it into your performance management system, so when you conduct performance reviews or even discuss performance informally, you can be very specific. You don't just make vague comments like, 'You're doing a great job, Jane,' or 'I'm not happy with your work, Joe.' You can refer specifically to the profile and say, 'These are the things I'm seeing, Jane, and I'm really happy about your performance! Keep it up!' *Or* you say, 'These are the attitudes and actions that I want to see, Joe, but I'm not seeing them right now. These are the specific areas where I'd like to you improve.'"

Dave rocks back in the chair and looks at Mike with a satisfied expression. "When we started talking, I mentioned the three key elements for business success: people, process, and product. We identified that you have a problem with your people model. Then we've laid out the system which will greatly advance the likelihood of hiring the right people—you **hire to a success profile**. If you're ready, I want to move on to the second element of improving your people: **Develop for performance and succession**. What do you say?"

Cottage Takeaways

- A system for people: hire to your success profile, develop for performance, and retain with engagement.
- In addition to skill, hire for aptitude and attitude.
- Success profile is a defined set of desired competencies and behaviors for each level of the organization:
    - Capabilities = What I do
    - Experience = What I've done
    - Personal attributes = Who I am
    - Knowledge = What I know
- Mike realizes he must live the model of the success profile.

Chapter Seven
"Develop for Performance and Succession"

"Dave, I'm really grateful to you for teaching me these concepts, but I have to tell you, I feel like I missed the mark. I've never done *any* of the things you've been telling me about. I never gave any *thought* to doing them!"

Dave gives Mike a warm smile. "I'd never thought about them either. It's not that I had deliberately avoided doing it, and I'm sure it's the same with you. It's just like you said, I had never really given it the proper thought, and that's because as a leader, one of the easiest things to do is to overlook the fundamentals."

Mike shakes his head wordlessly.

"Your dad was developing *you*," Dave continues, "and teaching you all the operational elements of the distribution business—how to do the work itself—picking and packing, operating and maintaining the equipment, getting the trucks in and out, inventory control, sales, supervision, and so on. Mike, you've swept the floors, you've done every job there is to do in that building. Am I right?"

Mike rolls his eyes, remembering back when he started. "Including cleaning the bathrooms."

Dave smiles. "Your father wanted you to know every aspect of the work that goes on in that building so that you would completely understand and fully relate to the challenges—*and* the joys—your employees experience every day. He was developing your skills as well as your understanding and empathy. I know he encouraged you to get your education so that you would have all the knowledge possible. He was working a systemic plan to complete your succession development and fully prepare you to be the owner of Stillwell Distributors one day. The last step was to give you this system that I'm explaining now." Sadness furrows Dave's brow as he sighs. "It just turned out that he didn't have as much time as he thought."

Mike's expression mirrors Dave's. "Yeah, he always said he was looking forward to my kids' college graduation."

"You know, your dad was the constant educator. He wanted you to fully grasp all the minutiae of operating a busy distribution center, then he planned to give you the overall, systemic view. That was the last step to complete before he retired and turned the company over to you. The good news is he shared his wisdom with me, and explained those three steps for successfully building your brand: **Hire to your success profile**, **Develop for performance and succession**, and

Retain the best people with engagement. Now I am honored to pass it along to you."

"So we've talked about creating success profiles and hiring to them, now let's look at the second element in the system." Dave sits up in his chair and taps the words he's written. "**Develop for performance and succession.** Are you ready to take some more notes?"

Mike grins and flips his notepad to a fresh page. "You bet!"

"OK, so if we hire to a success profile, you're going to hire someone who has all the attributes you're looking for, right? You'll hire someone your success profile indicates has a high likelihood of success. Their interviews and assessments confirm this person has good motor skills. They care about the quality of their work. They have integrity, loyalty, and are eager to learn. But maybe that person has only operated a Bobcat, not driven a fork truck. Could a person like that succeed at Stillwell Distributors?"

"Absolutely." Mike gives a firm nod.

Dave grins. "As a matter of fact, a person like that is far more likely to succeed than someone who has operated a fork truck for years, but doesn't meet any of the other elements of your success profile. So you've hired someone with the personal attributes you want. The next step is to intentionally instruct this individual and develop their skills as a fork truck driver."

"There's another scenario that belongs here, though."

Dave holds up the palm of his hand signaling a pause to emphasize his point. "As you move up your organizational chart, think about using the very same approach with a success profile designed for supervisors and managers. What system do you use for selecting and developing them?"

Mike frowns. "You keep using the word 'system,' Dave, and it makes my stomach clench because I don't *have* a system." He purses his lips and looks frankly at his uncle. "When an employee has good skills and wants to become a supervisor I have that person shadow Debbie, my most experienced employee. That way they can watch and learn."

Dave's face grows serious. "So the reality is the person you've just promoted has very little chance of ever being better than Debbie. Does Debbie tell the new managers what's expected of them? Or is it more like, 'Here's what I do every day'? What would Debbie be able to teach a new manager about using a success profile?"

Mike begins to drum his fingers pensively on the table again. "Until tonight, *I* wouldn't have been able to teach Debbie about using a success profile!"

Dave nods his understanding. "We're not simply talking about new hires or new promotions. Perhaps you have someone who was promoted years ago because of their proficiency at operations, but he or she needs to better demonstrate the attributes of your success profile. Do you have anybody like that?"

"Shoot, Dave." Mike gives his uncle a rueful smile. "I

don't need to stop and think about that. There are many who could improve their people skills, but I have to admit that even *I* need to improve my leadership skills."

"And, I *know* we've got some people—not just at the supervisory level—who were great individual contributors. We promoted them to the next level and expected them to be great there too. But the only 'development' we gave them—" Mike's voice places an ironic emphasis on the word *development*. "—was to expect them to figure it out on the job."

Shame creases Mike's face and his eyes squeeze shut for a moment in a pained expression. "My national sales manager is a man named Brad Harrington. Before I promoted him, he was our top sales rep four years running..." Mike's voice trails off and he stares up at the ceiling for a moment, shaking his head.

"I used to make a fuss over Brad all the time," Mike says softly. "I'd go on and on about him being our best, our stud salesman, our annual all-star." He looks back down at his uncle unhappily. "Since I promoted Brad, I don't think I've said one positive thing to him. All my conversations have been about what's wrong." Mike heaves a deep sigh. "And I never gave him *five minutes* of training!" He slaps his thigh in an angry gesture. "Here's your new office, Brad, you're in charge, now go out and double our sales."

"And today?" Dave gently asks.

"Today?" Mike's voice grows bitter because he's ashamed at how the situation has degenerated. "Now all he hears from me is, 'What's wrong with our sales numbers?' Brad works harder than he ever did, but all I tell him is how unhappy I am about the work he's doing." Suddenly, Mike's eyes widen in realization. "I bet he'd love it if we invested in some coaching for him on how to improve, rather than always grinding on him about poor performance."

Dave leans forward slightly. "Sounds as if someone like Brad—*if* he fits your success profile—would benefit tremendously from some performance development. Mike, when you get right down to it, *all* your employees need development of some type. As human beings, we're all a work in progress. Think about your own development. You've followed your father's succession plan since you were a young boy, right on through your MBA, and here you sit today, *still* learning and developing as you come to understand this system for success."

"Whether we're talking about an entry-level employee or an experienced leader, assuming they need no development is just not realistic." Dave smiles at Mike to take the sting out of his words. "That's especially true in today's world where not only does technology change so quickly, but the competitive landscape is more intense than ever before. The pressures of quality, customer service, and price are never going to get easier. The *healthiest organizations* focus on constant, continual development."

Mike nods in thoughtful agreement. "And I haven't been leading us in a very healthy way."

"That's because you didn't have the *system*," Dave says with a shrug. "There's a model for development that everyone goes through, or *should* go through, regardless of their level in your organization. All your employees should continuously develop their technical, their management, and their leadership skills."

"For example, Mike, consider a picker or a fork truck driver. I'm sure your inventory control system is constantly evolving and improving as you utilize the latest technology. Therefore, they should be developing their technical skills in managing your inventory system. In addition to that, they must exercise project management skills to organize their workflow, so they may need development in the area of productivity. And finally, leadership ability must be developed, such as their style of interpersonal communication and how they treat both internal and external customers in a way that's fully consistent with your company values."

Mike has been busily scribbling notes, but now he looks up at Dave with a curious expression. "Say that last part again? About internal and external customers?"

Dave thinks for a moment before he replies. "Let me put that to you in a different way. At what point do you teach your employees about what is expected of them when it comes to the customer?"

"I train my sales team," Mike replies promptly. "I sit with each sales rep when they're first hired and tell them how important our customers are to us."

"OK," Dave agrees. "That's a good start, but I want you

to start thinking more systemically than that. What *specifically* do you teach your employees about the customer relationships you expect at Stillwater Distributors?"

Mike flushes. "When you use that word 'specifically,' it makes me realize that maybe I've been a bit cliché. There are a lot of things I've emphasized over the years. You know, 'Treat customers right and they'll always come back'; or, 'The customer is always right'; and, 'The customer is king,' expressions like that."

"Do you have them written down?" Dave persists. "Do you have a manual with customer service principles written out for them to study and remember?"

Mike clears his throat uncomfortably. "Something else to add to my to-do list," he mutters, jotting a note.

"While you're thinking about how to present that information, Mike, think about asking and answering this question: '*Who is your customer?*' All too often, when employees hear the word 'customer,' they automatically think of people outside the building. But when we were talking about the concept of advancing your brand earlier, remember that your employees are *living* your brand! We discussed the systemic implications of the interactions between your forklift operator and a truck driver. That's just one simple example of customer service, but it's important to go back even further than that into the chain of customer service. What is the relationship between the picker and the forklift operator? How satisfied is the forklift driver with the customer service that he or she is receiving from the picker? Because that's going to impact the way that forklift operator interacts with the truck driver."

Mike stares at Dave intently. "You're right, I should be talking about customer service to *everybody all the time.*"

"*Now* you're thinking systemically!" Delighted, Dave reaches out and thumps his forefinger on the notepad for emphasis. "Many organizations only think of their 'customer service representatives' when they set up this kind of training. However, the elite organizations teach *everyone* how to deliver superior customer service to both their internal and external customers. It's an attitude."

Mike jots another note and looks at his uncle. "You're right again, Dave. I've been thinking for some time now that I should be doing more to develop our people. I just hadn't made it a priority and it wasn't clear to me how to do that."

Dave nods. "I'd have to say that developing the technical skills, as important as that is, is the easiest part of our development model. Teaching someone to operate a fork truck properly and safely is *essential,* yet relatively easy. When you start talking about teaching your pickers, drivers, and managers how to develop those interpersonal abilities that fall under the personal attributes of 'Who I Am' in the success profile, now you're talking about a more challenging task. Something you should think about, Mike, is how do you make the largest, long-term impact on your business results?"

Dave reaches for his own notepad and flips the pages back to his diagram of the success profile. "Take a look at this again."

Leadership	Success Profile
Capabilities • Lead change / Create Engagement • Relationships & Partnerships • Develop & Deploy a Vision • Achieve through People • Drive Performance What I Do	**Experience** • Internal & External Organization • Functions Worked • Accountability & Delivery What I've Done
Personal Attributes Who I Am • Emotional Intelligence • Professional Disposition • Drive to Achieve • Ownership / Integrity	**Knowledge** What I Know • Your Organization • Your Competitors • Key Business Processes • The world outside of your Business

The thoughtful look in Mike's eyes has been replaced by an expression of intense concentration. His excitement rising, he takes the notepad out of his uncle's grasp and begins scribbling notes.

After a moment of writing furiously, Mike says with confidence, "I get it. I can see my focus has to be balanced between all four quadrants. Focusing on one without the other is an incomplete approach; however, for some employees I may need to focus on one quadrant more than another. For example, Brad's strengths fall in the 'What I know' quadrant. That's why I promoted him. But looking at it holistically, he needs development in the 'What I do' and 'Who I am' quadrants. On the other hand, Debbie's strength is 'What I do.' She would benefit greatly from development in 'What I have done' and 'What I know,' because she has only worked for Stillwell. She simply doesn't have outside experience to draw upon."

Pleased at Mike's growing enthusiasm and confidence, Dave continues. "Do you see how we're continuing to work off the success profile? When you get to work Monday morning and you begin creating your success profile, you want to think in terms of development programs that will address each of these four quadrants. The elite companies are so committed to development that they offer training to *all* their employees in all four quadrants."

"One of the things we emphasized at my company, Mike, was training people in how to lead change and create engagement." Dave displays a wry smile. "I learned from bitter experience that we should never assume everyone instinctively knows how to create engagement. There's a prescription for it. Sure, there are those men and women who naturally possess more of those attributes and are more naturally disposed to creating engagement, but we cannot—*must* not—leave engagement to random chance. That won't create a healthy culture and it's *not* a healthy way to do business! So we put deliberate effort into teaching people how to lead change and create engagement, just as we taught all our supervisors how to drive and measure performance."

"So you see, Mike, this second step—develop for succession and performance—is not isolated from the first step of hiring to a success profile. Far from it! Even the third step, retain the best people with engagement, is entirely systemic in nature. But we'll talk more about the third step in a moment. There must be an order, a reason, and a progression. You have to achieve A before you can achieve B and C. So (A) you *create* the success profile, (B) develop interview questions from the success profile, and then (C) you *hire* to the success profile."

"Now that you're hiring employees using this model, you should consider what you're measuring. Until now, you have been managing to expectations that are tactical in nature, establishing key performance indicators such as punctuality, run times, delivery times, load times, accident-free...all part of the success profile. With the success profile, you can measure things that are less tangible, like leading change, working collaboratively within a team, ownership, and integrity. It's vital that you develop managers and leaders who know how to do this."

Mike nods vigorously. "I understand. That's a key component of systemic success."

"Exactly right!" Dave grins. "So coming back to your development system. You've *interviewed* according to the profile; you've *hired* based on the profile; you *evaluate* according to the profile; and finally, you *develop* to the success profile, intentionally creating programs that help your employees grow and improve in all four of these quadrants." Dave taps his diagram on the notepad for emphasis. "Now you see why shadowing Debbie probably isn't the best process. The last step is for you to *evaluate* according to the success profile. You teach your supervisors how to interpret, lead, and manage to it."

"Mike, when you put this system in place—and it *is* a system, each section linking to the other, each one building on the other, all sections working in sequence with each other—you're going to see positive results. You lay the foundation with the success profile to get the right people on the bus, as Jim Collins said. Then you invest in creating a development model for each group of employees—individual contributors, supervisors, managers, and senior leaders. You do these things, and the improvement you'll see at Stillwell Distributors will be absolutely dramatic!"

Mike is writing furiously, and Dave remains silent for a few beats, allowing his nephew to get caught up on his note-taking. Suddenly Mike slaps the pen down and grins. "I gotta tell you, for the first time in a long time I am really excited. I think we can *do* this!"

Dave laughs out loud, catching onto Mike's eagerness. "Well, don't go charging out the door just yet. It is getting late and we've got shingles to put on in the morning! Plus, there's one more element to the system I need to explain to you before we turn in for the night: **Retain with Engagement**."

Cottage Takeaways

- All employees need continuous professional development in alignment with the competencies and behaviors identified in the success profile.
- By developing employees, you create an organizational response that will create a higher individual response of engagement, commitment, and overall loyalty.
- Mike realizes the systemic process centered around the success profiles (in order):
  A. Create the success profile
  B. Develop interview questions from the success profile
  C. Hire to the success profile
  D. Develop to the success profile

Chapter Eight
"What's Your Promise?"

Mike grins and flips to yet another new page. "I want to hear more about retaining with engagement."

"Of course," Dave says. "After you've made the investment to identify the best people and develop them, you might do well to encourage them to stay." Dave's voice takes on a serious tone as he continues. "Now Mike, I'm afraid this next part of the system may be the most difficult for you to hear."

Mike frowns. "Why do you say that?"

"I'll talk to you in a minute about how you can measure the levels of engagement you have in your organization," Dave says carefully, his expression pensive. "That part is relatively simple. You use a survey analysis tool that helps quantify levels of engagement and identify those areas that you need to focus on."

Mike's eyes narrow as he starts to recall a memory from his early years on the job. "Dad used to conduct what he called 'Employee Engagement Surveys' with some regularity." Mike flushes and looks guiltily at his uncle. "I guess I thought that was a waste of time. I haven't done one since Dad passed away."

To Mike's surprise, Dave throws back his head and laughs. "That's exactly what I thought when your dad first brought up doing a survey to me! It seemed like just a bunch of pink fluffy stuff. Then he asked me what my employee turnover was like. That made me sit and start listening."

Mike sighs. "Yeah, I should have done more listening, too." His chagrinned expression acknowledges his own shortcomings as he looks down at the notepad. "Like you said, I still have a great deal of development to do on my own."

Dave's voice is very soft and serious as he says, "This engagement piece may very well be an area that will require the most development of all."

His words bring Mike's interested gaze up to his uncle's. "This is the hardest part of the system?"

"No, not necessarily," Dave replies. "But this is the piece of the system that requires you to take a long, hard look at yourself, because engagement starts with you...what you're doing...and what you're *not* doing."

Mike pushes out a short, sarcastic laugh at himself, recognizing his own short comings. "There have been plenty of things you've already shown me that I'm *not* doing! I can take it. Hit me with your best shot."

The edges of Dave's mouth slide up in a wry grin. "I don't want to hit you, but I may have to say a few things that sting a bit. It all comes back to the first element in the system: the success profile. The leaders in every organization have to carefully study the success profile. That's where it all starts...with *you*—" Dave points a finger at Mike "—CEO of Stillwell Distributors."

Mike looks at his uncle steadily. "Based on the volume of issues, I know I need to do things differently."

"The good news is that you don't have to guess how your people are feeling," Dave says. "Your dad didn't guess. You'll conduct employee engagement surveys so that you can quantify it. You already said your dad regularly did the same. That's Step One."

"Now, it's important to stop and emphasize right here that conducting the survey isn't the end. It's simply a *means* to the end of retaining with engagement. You conduct the survey every year or two and then analyze and address the results. But the survey itself doesn't retain with engagement, Mike. It's what you *do* with the results. In fact, if you conduct the survey and then do nothing with the results, you'll create more harm than good."

"I understand," Mike says. "It's like not giving any feedback to the suggestions in the 'Suggestion Box.' People start thinking, 'What's the point of sharing my ideas if no one is reading them?'"

"That's precisely right." Dave crosses his arms with a satisfied smile, pleased to see Mike catching on so quickly. "You actually create *dis*-engagement! So once you have the survey results, you can begin moving some things off the table as you zero in on the most important engagement issues for your organization. Here are three of those things that are relatively easy to address: you must be sure that your compensation, benefits package, and working conditions are fair and equal."

Mike jots three words on the notepad: **Compensation, Benefits, Work conditions.**

Compensation
Benefits
WORK Conditions
USE survey Data to make sure they are Competitive!
NO Guessing Here!

When Mike looks up, Dave continues. "One thing an employee engagement survey will tell you is how your staff feels about compensation and benefits. We talked about that earlier tonight, remember? You said you're not really sure if your pay and benefits are competitive. Right?"

"Yeah, that's right," Mike says on a disgruntled sigh.

"Stay with me here." Dave holds up a hand, as if to stem Mike's frustration. "What's even more important is finding out if your employees *believe* you're competitive. Here's the thing: you don't have to be the highest-paying employer in your city, but you do have to pay *competitively*."

"Let's say I'm an employee at Stillwell Distributors. If I'm like most people, I don't have to be the highest paid person at my position, but I do want you to pay me competitively. Same thing with the benefits package; you don't have to give me the Rolls Royce version of health plans, but if I find out that other companies are offering a Gold plan and I'm a Bronze plan, I'm going to be disgruntled. Most people expect competitive pay and benefits. Does that make sense?"

"Definitely," Mike says, rapidly jotting notes again. "If I hear Leland Distribution is paying forklift drivers $15.00 per hour and I'm only getting $14.50, that's not going to make me jump up and leave. But if I'm only getting $12.00, that's another matter altogether."

"That's it," Dave agrees. "Working conditions are just like that. I don't have to have a gym and a recreational room, but I *do* need a working environment that provides me with a *chance* to be engaged. If I'm working so hard that all I do is eat, sleep, and work...or if the workplace itself is cluttered and the equipment is substandard, I won't feel good about my job and I may start looking elsewhere."

"Hmm," Mike says thoughtfully, tapping the notepad with his pen. "I told you before about Ray, our maintenance supervisor who just left us to go work with one of our chief competitors. He said he wanted more time with his family; his main motivator was working less hours. With us, a 60-hour week was a short week. So he started looking around and found he could make a lot more money elsewhere...*and* work less hours."

"Exactly," Dave says emphatically. "If I believe I'm being paid a competitive wage and benefits, if I don't feel like I'm overwhelmed with work and the workplace isn't a dump, I'm *less* likely to consider other opportunities. But when pay, benefits, or working conditions start to feel like they're out of line, then I am *more* likely to consider other options."

"Let me give you a 'for instance.' Think about your warehouse and consider the message you're currently sending to your employees. When I visited last year and you gave me the tour, you showed me the lobby and the conference room, the places where you meet and greet customers. Those areas were very impressive. You've really made an investment in making those spaces clean, comfortable, and modern-looking."

Mike nods with satisfaction. "'Investment' is the right word. They say you only have one chance to make a good first impression. We see those rooms as being like a brochure for our customers, one that speaks of professionalism and leading technology. We spent a fair amount of money getting that right."

"That's good," Dave says. "You want to take every opportunity to 'Wow' your customers." He pauses, looking at Mike steadily. "But after you showed me the front end of the building, you took me in back to see the warehouse. We passed through the employee break room." Dave leans back in his chair and folds his arms across his chest, gazing steadily at Mike. "There was nothing 'Wow' about that break room. In fact, it didn't look like you've upgraded anything since your dad's time. Why do you invest so heavily in one area, but not in the other? There's quite a contrast between the two environments, and your employees see that contrast. I wonder how they feel about it."

Mike stiffens at the question and what it makes him realize. After a brief pause he sighs. "I hadn't given that any thought, Dave, and I certainly haven't asked. Like you say...I'm unintentionally sending a demotivating message."

"Yes, you are, but the good news is that you can easily *change* that message. Like I say, you start by taking a good, long look at the three things you can and should get off the table: pay, benefits, and the working environment. Conduct a formal compensation and benefit analysis that will answer a lot of those questions, and your employee engagement survey will tell you the rest."

"Sounds easy enough," Mike says agreeably.

"Because that *is* the easy part," Dave says drily. "But let's come back to the loyalty issue. You've mentioned it a couple of times today. If employees are disloyal to you, how do you flip that to create loyalty?"

Mike shrugs. "Well, before this conversation I used to think it was through pay and benefits. Now I'm wondering the real answer."

"In a word, *connection*. Ask yourself this: Why would someone choose to work for Stillwell Distributors?"

Mike takes some time to consider before answering. "We've always been a steady company...we've got lots of work...and we've never had a layoff—at least not yet."

Dave looks directly at Mike. "So someone should work for you because you offer steady employment? Nothing more?"

Mike looks confused.

"People don't want to just go to work. They want a way of life," Dave explains. "They want to be inspired and know how they're adding value. Sometimes those of us in leadership minimize how important work is to our employees and we forget that this is a *big* part of their lives that we're affecting. When you love what you do, believe that it's important and valuable, you'll be committed to the company's success."

"I get it." Mike speaks very slowly, like a man working through an intriguing puzzle. "People need to feel fulfilled by the work they do."

"You're on the right track!" Dave says, smiling. "Think back to what your company was like ten years ago—a few years before your father passed. What were your employees' attitudes like back then?"

"A lot different," Mike admits, his tone far from happy. "Everyone was positive and engaged. We worked hard, but we got things done right the first time—and everybody seemed to get along so well! There was a sense that everyone was a part of something bigger than just their job." Mike shakes his head and looks at his uncle with wounded eyes. "They were, to use your word, connected! I don't know how I've let us get so far away from that."

Dave shrugs, his lips tipped in a conciliatory smile. "You were probably working so hard to build the business you didn't realize what was happening. That's how it was with me. Mike, you said something earlier about your company having a 'reputation for dysfunction.' Reputations are built on fulfilling your promise…or not. You've made promises to your customers, and evidently some customers are unhappy because those promises haven't been kept. What about your employees? What's your promise to them?"

"My promise?" Mike draws back in surprise. He thinks for a long moment before he replies, "Well…we are working hard to keep the business growing. We provide them with plenty of work…" His voice trails off. "But as I listen to you talk, I don't know that we really *do* make any promise, other than that they'll get a paycheck, health insurance, and at least forty hours a week. It's become clearer to me that if I'm going to attract and retain the best people, it needs to be much more than that."

"That's right. Think of the moment when you're hiring a new employee and you look that individual directly in the eye. What promise are you making to him or her? You're saying, 'If you come to work at Stillwell Distributors, I promise you...' Now finish that sentence."

His expression bleak, Mike gazes back at his uncle. "I have to admit I don't know how I'd finish it."

"Being able to answer this question and express it to everyone who works for you is critical," Dave says. "You may have to do some soul searching and take an honest look at what you're promising your employees and how you're going to live up to it. Elite employers can answer this question and they build the system we just discussed around it. The promise is the foundation for everything we discussed tonight."

Mike shuffles through the notepad and locates the success profile page:

"In the upper-left corner," Dave continues, "the 'What I Do' quadrant, you see that the first responsibilities are **lead change and create engagement,** followed by **build relationships and partnerships**."

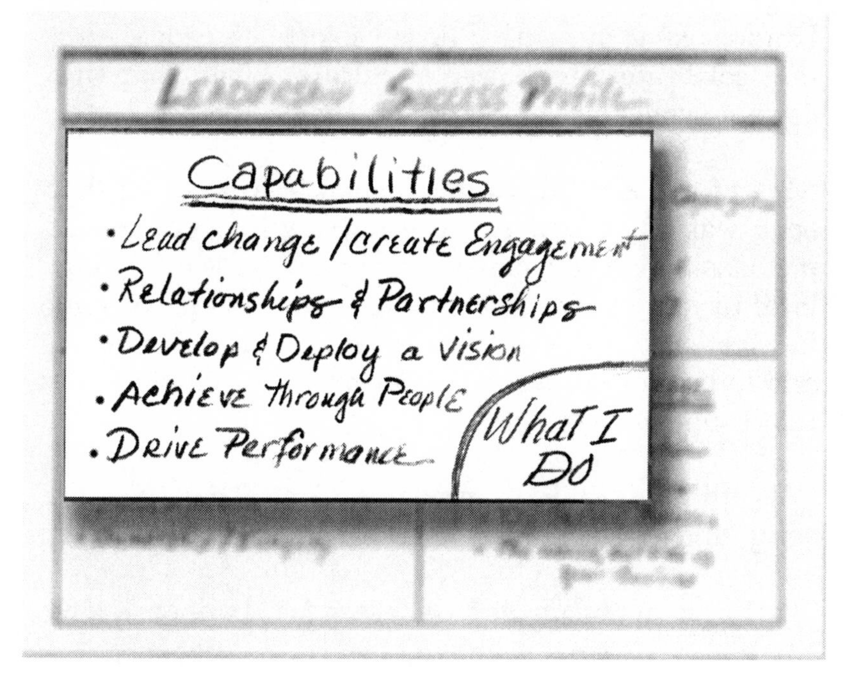

Mike stares intently at the success profile diagram. "I'd have to tell you that we talk about exactly *none* of these things in our management meetings," he says flatly.

Dave nods sympathetically. "That certainly doesn't make your company unique. When your dad first showed me these concepts, I thought my entire job was to find new work, make sure crews got to all the jobs on schedule, and follow up to be sure our clients were satisfied. I was pleasant enough to our workers, I suppose, but in terms of working intentionally to create engagement or build internal partnerships? It never entered my mind!"

"So what did you do, Dave?"

"I talked with your dad about creating engagement at great length. A few years ago, a man named Jack Lannom came out with a little book called *People First* that celebrates the power of culture. Write that title down on your to-read list, Mike: *People First*."[1]

"One of the key takeaways for me from reading that book was this: **You can't impart what you don't possess**. You said you want your employees to be more loyal to your organization, more committed to working in excellence, to get along smoothly with each other, and to be more proactive about problem solving. Does that sound right?"

"Yes, that's it," Mike agrees readily. "That's what I want, and all that seems to be lacking right now."

"This area of engagement is where Mr. Lannom's idea

1 Jack Lannom, *People First* (Pembroke Pines, FL, Grace World Publishing ©2003-2015).

becomes a stark reality," Dave replies. "He teaches that *you can't impart what you don't possess.* If you as a leader want your employees to be loyal, committed, harmonious, and resourceful, what are you doing to model those qualities for them?"

Mike sets his pen down carefully on the notepad and looks at Dave quizzically. "'Model' those qualities?"

"Yes! Do your employees see and sense your loyalty *to them?* Do they see and sense your commitment to *their* success? Do they see and sense a strong spirit of harmony among your leadership team?" Dave rests his arms on the table and leans toward Mike. "Are your leaders building strong relationships and partnerships within your organization? When they're confronted with an issue, do they pull the team together to devise the best solution?"

The silence seems to stretch out for an uncomfortably long time. Finally, Mike shakes his head slowly, shocked by the realizations he is making. "As much as I hate to admit this, I think I'd have to answer all those questions, 'No.'"

"So, if your employees don't see these qualities that you desire modeled by you and your leadership team, it's going to be difficult for them to engage in behaviors that are somewhat unfamiliar to them. Is that a reasonable assumption?"

Mike purses his lips and then pushes out a long, unhappy breath of air. "You said this part of the system might be the most difficult to hear. You were right!"

"That's actually good to know. It means you're ready to move in the right direction." Dave taps his notepad with an open palm. "Let's talk about how to begin making some positive changes in this area. You've said you want certain things from your employees. You also said you want your employees to know there are certain things you'd like to provide for them. When I asked you what you wanted your business to look like, you said you wanted your employees to know that you wanted them to succeed—not just in the workplace, but also in their personal lives. Correct?"

"Absolutely!"

"So how do you *demonstrate* that desire?"

Confused, Mike shakes his head. "Ask me that question again?"

"It's really just a different way of asking you the question I posed a moment ago: *What is the promise that you make to your employees?* Mike, it's entirely reasonable for you to expect the things you're asking from your people: loyalty, commitment, a cordial workplace, and a proactive attitude toward problem-solving. That's their promise to you. You said that right now, your only promise to them is basically that they'll get a paycheck and benefits. Right?"

Mike nods.

"Thirty years ago, that was a good promise. 'You'll get a paycheck that will clear. When you go to the doctor, they'll accept your health insurance.' That was the promise that was made to me and your father when we were young."

"But a lot has changed in the last few decades. Today we *expect* that the check will clear. We *expect* health coverage. We *expect* a workplace that's in compliance with all state and federal regulations, including safety. That's the bare minimum! All employees today, even your most senior employees, want a lot more than that. They want a compelling promise from you. In essence, they want you to answer the question 'What's in it for me?'"

"Mike, at lunchtime today we were talking about our construction project and you referred to the addition as a 'house' for Aunt Rita. I stopped you right away and said we should think of it as a 'home,' not just a 'house.' Remember?"

Mike nods, looking at Dave intently.

"Your employees are just like Aunt Rita. They don't want just a house. They want a *home.* They're not just looking for a job; they're looking for a way of life. They want to know that they're making a meaningful contribution to a successful enterprise. Just about anybody can have a house, but many people enjoy living in a *home*—a place of warmth and connection. In the very same way, just about anybody who wants to can find a job that offers a paycheck and benefits, but they're longing for something more. They want a career. They're looking for a way of life."

Dave stops speaking and looks at Mike curiously for

a moment. "So what's your promise to your employees? Why should they choose to work for you? What's in it for them? You can be sure they want to know."

Mike drops his gaze and considers his notes. "I see your point, Uncle Dave," he says with a sigh. "That's a question I need to be able to answer."

Dave nods and smiles as he watches Mike writing in his notepad again. "That's right, but don't get down on yourself. I couldn't answer that question when your father first asked me. You'll discover it."

"You know what? I think I will." Mike's voice sounds stronger and his expression grows hopeful. "You've been using this word 'systemic' a lot, and I'm beginning to see why. All these different elements are interconnected with each other. It's not about doing one or two of these things, even though each one is important. It's doing all of them together that will bring about sustainable success."

Dave nods as he says, "I'll come back to the *People First* book one more time. The last point I want to share is how Jack Lannom says that **each and every person in your organization—regardless of what their job title is, needs to know that who they are and what they do has meaning and significance**. One of the chief responsibilities of every leader is to help each employee make those connections, show them that the effort, energy, and diligence they bring to work is making a direct impact on success. You find ways to celebrate those successes! You say you want people in your company to get along better. One of the best ways to make that happen is to show them how their hard work is making life better—not just for them personally, but for the whole organization *and* for your external customers."

Mike has stopped writing and is looking intently at Dave. "Whereas if work is only about picking up a paycheck, their attitude is *much* more likely to be 'Every man for himself.'"

Dave smiles warmly. "You've got this! You work to create a culture which is based on success, but it's much greater than that. It's a culture that retains the best people with engagement because you're creating a culture of belonging, a culture where people feel like they share in your successes."

Mike grins happily as he jots down more notes. "I have to tell you, Uncle Dave, I'm actually *excited* to get back to work!"

"But you've got a big problem staring you square in the face when you get back, don't you?"

Mike's smile vanishes and he glances up at Dave quickly. "Problem?"

Dave looks at Mike steadily. "Your phone call at lunchtime today. From what I could hear of your end of the conversation, your company was late on a delivery, and it wasn't the first time this has happened. If I heard right, you were forced to make all kinds of concessions in order to keep the account, and it's one of your biggest accounts."

"It's our single biggest biller," Mike says grimly. "Losing that one account could put me out of business. It would mean major layoffs at the very least."

"OK, so here's the perfect opportunity to put some of these ideas we've been talking about tonight to work. Someone who doesn't follow this system would likely go charging into the office and start barking at people about how they need to get their act together or lose their jobs, that kind of stuff. But you're going back to work with the goal of developing your employees and retaining with engagement. So rather than stomping in and putting the fear of layoffs into them, you're thinking about, '*How am I going to engage and rally our workforce to meet this crisis?* I *must* do something different, or we're going to keep getting what we've always gotten.'"

Mike nods, his expression sober. "You can say that again."

"It doesn't mean that you sugarcoat the severity of the problem. You tell your team exactly where you stand at present. You say, 'Right now we're on a course that will cause us to lose this game, however, we're going to work together to devise a process that's different from what we've done in the past. It's a process that will be visible and measurable, and we're going to celebrate together when we win!'"

Dave is silent for a moment, and Mike glances up from his notes. "OK, tell me about the process."

Dave shakes his head and grins widely. "I don't know

the process, Mike. Remember, I was just a simple landscaper!"

Both Dave and Mike laugh aloud.

Then Dave grows serious again, though his eyes are bright with conviction. "But *you* know the process. You and your team. I would encourage you to pull together the people who are closest to the work and get their full input and collaboration on developing a solution. Ask them what's working and what's not. Ask them where the breakdowns take place and where the bottlenecks are. Ask them if there are areas where they feel disempowered. If any of the things they identify as needing improvement are things that you yourself put in place, Mike, don't get defensive! Thank them for pointing out what's not working and involve them in creating a viable solution as well as the measures you'll use to ensure the solution is functioning properly."

Mike gives his uncle a crooked grin. "So if I'm going to *talk* about engagement, I should actually engage our employees in the solution process."

"Most definitely!" Dave says firmly. "That doesn't mean you surrender your role as the leader. There's a management element that is yours and yours alone—" here Dave ticks the points off on his fingers "—emphasizing your values, communicating goals and expectations, monitoring the progress to reaching those goals, making sure that everyone is staying on track, and celebrating the efforts people are making toward reaching success. You *can't* delegate those things, Mike, and you can't ignore them."

"Can I call you if I'm floundering?" Mike asks, grateful for his uncle's mentorship.

"You can call me any time of the day or night. I mean that! If your phone rings at 2:00 a.m. and you need me, call. But I really don't think you'll need to do that because this system we've laid out for you *works.* It worked for your father, it worked beautifully for me, and I am positive it's going to work for you as well. You retain the best people with engagement by creating a culture of belonging. Belonging to the promise you'll make to every one of your employees."

"You said you can see the system, Mike. You've got to hire to the success profile so you have the right people in your company who resonate with what you're trying to do; then you develop those people. You develop leaders who will lead this change and create engagement with your employees. Leaders who will build relationships and partnerships—both internally and externally. Some people are more naturally disposed to that than others, so you're going to have to help some of your leaders develop those abilities. Perhaps the most important way to do that is by *you* being a very visible model of that development."

"You're always working on this third element," Dave continues. "Retaining the best people with engagement; it never goes on autopilot. You make sure you're compensating employees fairly—not necessarily the *most*, but definitely in line with your competitors. You strive to make the working conditions such that people are willing to engage. You monitor employee engagement through regular employee surveys. Finally, you keep people informed and get them involved. From what you've told me and what I've heard on your phone calls, this may be something you'll need to really concentrate on. You told me your phone is always ringing and you feel like you have to do everything yourself. Maybe that's because your leaders and managers don't feel like they're fully in the loop."

"Everything you need to help you succeed is laid out here." Dave spreads his hands to indicate their two notepads, then leans back in his chair and heaves a deep, satisfied sigh. "That's the system that will take you and Stillwell Distributors to success."

By now it's almost midnight and the moon is high over the pond. Dave and Mike are both tired and ready to turn in. Mike looks across the table at his uncle, his face showing relief as the weight he's been carrying for years finally seems to be lifting. "Uncle Dave, thank you. You and my father were absolutely right, it's simple, yet complicated...'leadership is simply complicated.'"

The next morning, Dave and Mike got an early start on finishing the roof of the cottage. In typical Dave fashion, he even had a process for applying the roof shingles. He had their tool belts and safety harnesses ready, all the required tools staged in the right place, and each bundle of shingles staged for efficient distribution and installation. By late afternoon, they had completed their task – the roof was done! After all the tools and extra materials were put away, Dave and Mike stood shoulder-to-shoulder on the front lawn to admire their handiwork. Both felt a tremendous sense of pride and satisfaction knowing they had helped Aunt Rita and created for her a new home.

Throughout that day, Mike reflected on everything he had learned from his wise Uncle. He knew what had to be done, and that a great challenge lies ahead of him. However, he was also excited about what the future might bring, and couldn't wait to get started!

Cottage Takeaways

- Use survey analysis tools to help quantify levels of engagement and identify those areas on which you need to focus.
- Compensation, benefits, and working conditions must be competitive. Validate they are competitive and share results with employees so they do not have to guess or do their own research.
- Employees want to feel a connection with the workplace. People don't want to "just go to work," they want a way of life. Create engagement by creating an environment of belonging.
- You can't impart what you don't possess. If a leader wants employees to be loyal, committed, harmonious, and resourceful, then the leader must possess those qualities.
- Every person in your organization needs to know what they do has meaning and significance.
- The Promise. Mike realizes he has not fulfilled his responsibility as the leader. He expects more from his employees than what he is giving. He must reflect and discover his promise to his employees. He must complete this statement: I, Mike Stillwell, promise every employee . . .

Epilogue

"No Longer Leading by the Seat of My Pants"

It's another beautiful day...but I feel so different!

Mike can't help but reflect on the dramatic difference in his frame of mind between today and the last time he made the drive to his Uncle Dave's home. Last October he had been sitting alone in the Explorer, filled with angst. Today Mike's wife, Lee Anne, is sitting next to him and their three teenagers are in the back seat, absorbed in the electronic world of their smartphones.

Mike glances at his phone, which is settled in the Explorer's console. They are only minutes from Dave's home, yet his phone has not rung once. Mike chuckles deep in this throat and looks over at Lee Anne. "I was just thinking about driving out here last fall to help Dave with the addition for Aunt Rita's new home. I was so stressed!"

Lee Anne smiles at her husband. "As I recall, you didn't want to make the trip at all."

"I didn't," Mike readily agrees. He shakes his head, grinning. "Who would have thought that a weekend I wished to avoid would have made such an impact on the business and our lives."

Lee Anne reaches over and gently squeezes her husband's arm. "Look at us. Headed out for a four-day weekend as a family. I was beginning to think we were never going to do anything like this again."

"At the rate I was going last year, you had every reason to worry about that," Mike says, his expression serious. "And I know I wasn't any fun to be around for quite some time." Mike covers his wife's hand with his own. "Thanks for putting up with me."

She smiles at Mike. "Uncle Dave is going to get a lot of extra hugs this weekend!"

The big oak tree marking Dave's driveway comes into view, and Mike calls back over his shoulder to his kids, "We're just about there!"

He looks at the old oak again and remembers. *The last time I saw that tree, I stopped the car. Can you imagine how bad life might be by now if I had turned around and gone back to work?*

Filled with gratitude and excitement, Mike pulls into the driveway and the cottage comes into view. The pond sparkles in the afternoon sun and the cottage looks comfortable and inviting. *I know how Lee Anne feels,* Mike thinks. *Shoot, I might give Uncle Dave a few hugs myself!*

Mike parks the Explorer and the family piles out. Dave comes out of the cottage to greet them, his eyes sparkling with genuine pleasure.

True to her word, Lee Anne steps forward and embraces Dave. "We're so happy to see you!" she says happily. "It's been *much* too long."

Mike hangs back for a moment, looking up at the addition to the cottage he helped build last year. Dave has stained the wooden siding in such a way that the new and the old sections of the home blend together beautifully. One would have to look closely to see that new work has been done. Mike can see his Aunt Rita sitting on the porch, enjoying the summer sunshine. She looks much thinner than Mike had remembered and makes no effort to walk down the porch stairs, but she does rise from her chair to wave a cheerful greeting. Mike smiles and waves back.

Dave is chatting with Mike's children, marveling at how much they've grown. Dave then shifts his attention to Mike and lifts his chin in an inquiring gesture that asks, "How are you?"

Mike's face splits into an enormous smile.

Dave excuses himself from the children and approaches Mike, smiling, his expression inquisitive. "You look five years younger than you did ten months ago! What did you do, find the fountain of youth?"

Without thinking about it, Mike envelops his uncle in a crushing hug. "We're doing great, Uncle Dave, and it's all thanks to you and your success system." Mike pulls back slightly, keeping his hands on his uncle's shoulders. "I've got so much to tell you. You won't believe how well things are going."

Dave grins and grips Mike's arms. "Let's get everyone settled and spend some time with Rita, then you can tell me all about it. I can't wait."

Two hours later, Dave and Mike are seated comfortably on some lawn chairs in the front yard, enjoying the warm, late afternoon sun. Mike's sons and daughter are happily paddling around the pond in Dave's canoe, and Lee Anne has gone inside with Aunt Rita.

Dave finally asks how the company is doing.

Mike leans back in his chair and smiles up at the clear summer sky. "Dave," he says warmly, "I typed out the notes I took when I was here with you last year, and I still review them once a week. Over time, those notes have expanded as I've answered some of the questions you told me I'd have to figure out for myself, but I always keep your original words highlighted because I want to make sure I stay on track. I looked over those notes last night before I came up here, because I wanted to be very clear about taking you, point-by-point, through what we've done in these last ten months. The very first thing I wrote down underneath the diagram you drew was, *'A system for people that will advance our brand.'*"

Mike shakes his head, and an expression of wonderment crosses his face. He smiles at his uncle. "I remember being hopeful when I wrote those words down, wishing you would give me a nudge in the right direction. Honestly, I had no idea you were opening a door that would allow me to enter a whole new world of excellence."

Mike raises a hand, his palm facing his uncle. "Now, please don't hear me saying that I think I've 'arrived' by any means. I still have a lot to learn and a lot to do, but the change in just ten months, Dave...you can *feel* it! The atmosphere in our offices and out on the warehouse floor is noticeably different, and it's not because we've been blowing a lot of people out the door and hiring new ones. Granted, we've had to make some personnel changes, but nowhere near as many as I'd thought we would. You know the old saying: 'It's easier to change your people than to change your people.' There's a whole new attitude at Stillwell Distributors."

Dave's eyes are bright with curiosity. "This sounds great! Tell me more."

Mike looks out over the pond for a moment, making sure his children are still seated safely in the canoe, then turns back to Dave. "I had some really pressing issues facing me the moment I walked back into the office after our weekend together. We had just lost a really valuable employee, one large account had cancelled, and our biggest customer had essentially told us that one more mistake would mean the end of *that* account. That would have been devastating for us. So we had people problems *and* process problems, but you told me to start with the people and that's exactly what I did."

"First thing Monday morning, I called all my senior leaders in for a meeting." Mike grins, remembering that day. "You could tell when they came in they were unhappy. In the past every time I'd called a meeting like that, it was to chew them out or announce the latest crisis. Well, we sure enough had a crisis, but I told them the biggest reason for it was me. I said I had basically been leading by the seat of my pants rather than following any kind of a leadership system."

"That took guts, Mike!" Dave says, impressed by his nephew's honesty. "How did they react?"

"I think they were a little taken aback," Mike answers. "I don't know that any of them had ever heard me say 'I was wrong' about anything...ever! A couple of them were looking at me strangely."

"So they were resistant?" Dave asks.

"'Cautious' might be a better description," Mike says, recalling the expressions on the senior leaders' faces. "Maybe they were cautiously optimistic. I'm sure some of them were thinking, 'This too shall pass.' But I had stayed up late the night before, talking with Lee Anne about your system and planning what I wanted to accomplish that morning. I really wanted to lay a firm foundation for action from the beginning. So I went to the whiteboard and laid out the three points of the system: **Hire to your success profile**, **develop for performance and succession**, and **retain the best people with engagement**. I explained to them in detail what those three points mean, and told them I would need their help in initiating all three elements of the system."

"You didn't waste any time!" Dave marvels. "How was their buy-in?"

"I was pleased at their response. Lee Anne and I had discussed how I needed to emphasize this system was just as new to me as it was to them, and that I would need to take the lead in modeling the system, not just talking about it. I asked all of them to hold me accountable, that if I slipped back into leading like the 'old Mike'" Mike pauses, recognizing a truth he can no longer deny. "I guess '*reacting*' would more accurately describe how I used to operate, but I asked them to call me on it right away if I fell back into my old ways. I admitted that I had done a terrible job of empowering them to make decisions, and did my best to reassure them that the first thing I wanted to do, that very morning, was empower them to help me stay on track with this new system."

Dave grins with sheer delight. "They *had* to be impressed with that."

Mike nods. "That's when I could feel them coming on board. I mean, it's not like I was a harsh dictator suddenly turning into Mother Theresa. I had a decent relationship with all of them, but it's gotten a lot better now. I've also discovered a 180-degree feedback tool that ensures they have the opportunity to provide candid feedback, which helps me hold myself accountable."

"That's outstanding, Mike!"

"So we got to work, right there that morning. I had already developed my promise. I'll tell you about that in a moment. We had lost a key person, our maintenance manager, so I put your success profile up on the whiteboard and we created three success profiles: one for individual contributors, one for those who manage or supervise, and one for the leadership team. Everybody enjoyed doing that, especially as they began to see the implications for people they would be hiring in their own departments." Mike looks at Dave gratefully. "That one step, Dave, creating a success profile, has made *such* a big difference for us."

Dave is leaning comfortably back in his chair, smiling at Mike with genuine pleasure.

"I've been looking forward to sharing the news with you." Mike gazes out at the pond again and nods with satisfaction as he sees the canoe returning back toward the cottage. "Here's one of the first bonuses that came from the work we started that morning. Later that day I sat down with Ray Weir, our maintenance manager who had just given us his notice. I'm sure he thought I was going to lay some kind of a guilt trip on him and pressure him to stay, because losing him was a big hit for us." Mike laughs as he recalls his conversation with Ray. "If I thought my leadership team was looking at me strangely..." Mike laughs with gusto. "Ray actually said to me, 'Mike, what's gotten into you?'"

"How did you answer him?" Dave asks, his curiosity growing.

"I didn't want to insult him by making some pitch about 'Please stay, we need you!' So I sat him down and thanked him for his years with us, but I also apologized to him for how things have been the last few years. I thanked him because Ray turning in his notice was part of a gigantic wake-up call for me, a call that made me realize the type of leader I had been. That led directly to my apology, which was that our company had worked him so hard he felt his only solution was to leave after seventeen years with us. I told him the fault for that was all mine, and I was quite sure that if Dad was still alive, things would never have gotten to this point. I said I was truly sorry that I hadn't spoken to my Uncle Dave earlier and come face-to-face with what I was doing wrong."

"So you say he was looking at you strangely, huh?" Dave asks drily.

Mike grins. "At that point, I think Ray was still waiting for me to say, 'What will it take to get you to stay?' So he was just blown away when I explained your system to him and asked for his input on the success profile. I told him his input would be invaluable—not only for the success profile, but also that he could help us create a culture of engagement that would keep us from burning out his replacement. I told Ray that we couldn't afford to lose more good people like him and I was hoping he'd help me see where we could make positive changes."

"Mike, you really hit a home run on your first day!" Dave says, his expression beaming with pride.

"Long story short," Mike concludes cheerfully, "Ray had given us three-week's notice. At the end of the second week, Ray came to my office and asked if we could talk about him staying on. He said he could see a definite change in me and he was feeling really engaged with what we were doing. He said he wanted to be a part of helping us with the systemic changes we were making.

We had already done some research on what it would cost to hire his replacement, and it turned out that the other company had made him a competitive offer for compensation. We *thought* we were paying Ray a fair wage, but we found out we weren't. So we matched the offer Ray had received and he's still with us."

Dave laughs aloud with sheer delight. "Outstanding! Retaining with engagement went to work for you right away."

"It's *all* working for us, Dave," Mike says warmly. "It's an outstanding success system. You told me to get those things off the table that would impede our efforts to create a positive culture—pay, benefits, and working conditions. I was really being honest with Ray. I felt very badly about what we had done to make him so unhappy, and I wanted his help in creating a working environment for his replacement that wouldn't make *that* person start looking for a new job. For Ray, we had been demanding *way* too many hours for too little pay. We took those two things off the table." Mike snaps his fingers and grins. "And today we've got a very happy employee."

"That's just tremendous, Mike!"

"I'm getting ahead of myself a little bit," Mike replies. He is excited to share all this news with his uncle and his thoughts are racing. "There were two other big wins that came out of that first day back to work after being here with you, Dave. I remember telling you about Brad Harrington, our national sales manager. You were talking to me about development, and I told you that I had promoted Brad because he was a great salesman, but I'd done nothing to help him develop into a great sales manager, or even a *competent* sales manager, for that matter."

"Well, when I was with all our leaders, I asked them to start thinking about how we would build a development system in our organization. I explained how this would run off the success profiles: first, we would have to identify how successful employees at Stillwell Distributors think and perform, and then we could work on helping them develop in those areas. No more of this, 'Just follow Debbie around for a week.' We've been working on it ever since that first day and we've made big strides in developing impactful learning programs at Stillwell Distributors."

"Way to go!"

"I asked Brad to stay after the meeting," Mike continues. "He was visibly apprehensive because we'd had all these problems with large accounts in recent days: one lost, our biggest customer threatening to leave. I'm sure he thought I was getting ready to grind on him about those things, maybe even fire him." Mike shakes his head slowly, remembering his previous behavior. "It's probably what I *would* have done if I hadn't talked to you, Dave. So you can imagine Brad's mouth was practically hanging open when I told him that out of all the people at our company who deserved an apology from me, he was the one whom I *most* needed to ask for forgiveness. I had promoted him, demanded nothing but excellence from him, and yet I had done absolutely *nothing* to develop him."

Mike sighs, still ashamed at how badly he had let things get. "I *still* can't believe I failed him that badly."

"You don't know what you don't know, Mike," Dave says in a firm, quiet voice. "As soon as you learned that there was a better way, you immediately took steps to change." Dave's face lights up with pride and joy. "On your very first day back! How has Brad been doing since?"

His uncle's praise lightens Mike's mood again. "Brad and I sat down the next day and created a success profile. We'd never done anything like that before. His only directive from me was 'Double our sales!' So we used your four quadrants to identify the skills, behaviors, and experience that we would want in a leader, if we were hiring one. There were several things on the success profile that Brad had no idea I was expecting, because I had never communicated them to him. Somehow I just assumed he knew what I wanted. We cleared away *so* much frustration and misunderstanding in that first meeting! Then we reviewed the quadrants and identified which attitudes and actions were strengths for him and which ones were areas for development. I ended up hiring a business coach to mentor Brad and help him develop those areas where he still needed to grow."

Mike looks at Dave with a smile. "Brad's team has been hitting it out of the park these last six months. Gross sales are up 15% from this time last year. Like all of us, Brad has been working hard to create that culture of engagement. Our sales team is feeling *much* better about themselves and about representing us. You don't even have to ask Brad how he's doing—you can see it on his face. He feels competent and confident again, like he did back in those days when he was our top sales rep."

Mike's kids pull the canoe up on shore. He smiles and waves at them, then looks back at Dave. "Brad is another one—another one like Ray Weir—I deserved to lose. It was your system that showed me how to put the plan in place that turned both those situations around. I can't thank you enough."

"I may have shown you the system," Dave says warmly, "but you were the one who implemented it, and you did it *really* well. I am so very proud of you!"

Mike reaches over and gently grips his uncle's forearm. "But there's something else I wanted to tell you. I saved the best for the last. I told you our operations people have created new systems for just about every aspect of our work, so we've become much more efficient in the way we service our accounts. This shift got started during that first morning meeting. I told all our leaders we had come within an eyelash of losing Top Technical, our most important account. I confessed that me holding meetings and telling them to 'Tighten up!' wasn't helping. We needed to work together to develop a process that would reduce our mistakes. A darn near foolproof process because we simply couldn't have one more breakdown in our service with Top Technical."

"Debbie, our first shift operations manager, suggested we get some of our warehouse people involved—the people who actually do the work—to help us identify breakdowns and bottlenecks. Then Brad Harrington asked what I thought about getting the customer involved, so we could hear directly from them what aspects of our service were working for them and where their pain points were. Brad said our customer would be an invaluable resource in creating the best systems."

"I reached out to Sarah Short, Top Technical's VP of Operations. You may remember I was on the phone with her getting reprimanded for our late delivery the first morning I was here with you, Dave. I was afraid Sarah would tell me to figure it out for myself, but she said she'd be delighted to get one of her managers involved in the process, and she sent one of her best. He was tremendously engaged and helpful to our team, not only by making improvements in all aspects of our service to them, but to all our other customers as well."

Dave grins with satisfaction. "So you've been able to hold on to that account?"

"It's even better than that, Dave." Mike's eyes light up with excitement. "One of the reasons our sales are up so dramatically is because Sarah Short referred two new companies to us in the past six months. She told them both that Stillwell is the most responsive and responsible distributor she's currently working with."

"Wow!" Dave draws back in surprise. "That's incredible news."

Mike smiles, nodding his head in agreement with his uncle. "Can you imagine that? Ten months ago I was telling you what a dysfunctional organization we were.

Sarah Short told me straight out that we were incompetent. Now, she's sending us business! We're getting back to how it was when Dad was there. New business is finding us. It's wonderful! We were at risk less than a year ago; now we're growing *and* improving systemically so we can handle that growth well."

"But the thing I'm *most* proud of is the looks I see on people's faces as I walk through our building. I do a lot more management by walking around than I did ten months ago. I talk to our employees a lot more than I used to. They're happy to be there and everyone is getting along so much better. Your success profile has helped us make some excellent hires, but I think the biggest change is the work that all our leaders and managers have done to build a culture that people *want* to be a part of. That had to start with me, just like you said, Uncle Dave, and I've worked hard to instill that mindset in all our leaders. And they've really responded. They're all on board with our promise."

Dave's eyes widen with interest. "Your promise?"

"Yes," Mike says. "Remember, you told me I needed to figure out what my promise was to our employees... something more than 'Work hard and get a paycheck.'" Mike's voice takes on a tone of playful severity. "You wouldn't help me with that one at all."

Dave grins, nodding in recollection. "No, I wouldn't. That one had to come straight from your heart."

"You were right," Mike says, both his tone and expression serious. "The promise had to come from me. I knew what I wanted to say, but I couldn't figure out how to distill it. I wanted it to be short and to the point, easily understood. Of all the things you taught me last year, Dave, I wrestled with this one the most. I wanted to get it just right, and for some reason it wasn't coming to me."

Mike raises his voice and calls to his fifteen-year-old daughter. "Maria, could you come here for a moment, honey?" Mike turns back to Dave. "I thought about it and thought about it. We'd talk about it as a family over dinner."

Mike's daughter Maria, a tall attractive girl with big brown eyes, joins them. Mike stands and puts his arm around her waist, pulling her to his side in an affectionate hug. She smiles at Dave gratefully. "Thank you so much for letting us use the canoe, Uncle Dave! I just *love* being out on the water."

"You're welcome, sweetheart," Dave says cheerfully. "If you'd like, maybe tonight we can go out for some night-fishing."

Maria looks at Mike eagerly. "May I?"

Mike gives his daughter a squeeze. "Of course. I also wanted you to help me tell this last part of how Uncle Dave's system has changed our company." Mike grins at his daughter before turning his attention back to Dave. "She's already informed me that she's taking over the business when I retire. She comes in after school and helps out in our HR department. Her brothers want to pursue engineering, but Maria says there have been men running Stillwell long enough. She believes it's time for a woman's touch."

Both Mike and Dave chuckle as Maria gives them a saucy grin.

"I've been taking my own development very seriously," Mike continues. "Reading a lot more and looking for opportunities to interact with other business leaders. Early this year I heard a man speak at a business event in our city. He's the CEO of a multinational corporation. I was really impressed with his leadership philosophy, but he said something about halfway through his presentation that really grabbed me. In fact, I don't think I heard anything else he said after that. It was like a light switch went on. *This was it!* Our promise. It was exactly what I'd been wanting to say, but he had thought it through and boiled it down to one sentence. I went home and shared it with Lee Anne and our future CEO—" Mike gives Maria a playful wink— "and they both liked it as much as I did. I gave it to our leadership team the next day, and they're 100% on board. It's our promise to our employees."

Dave is gazing at Mike intently. "So what is it?"

"I wanted Maria to tell you, Uncle Dave. I know my father was doing everything he could to develop me, but he didn't get around to giving me the systemic picture. I'm so grateful you were here to do that for him, but I don't want to take a chance on Maria missing out on this knowledge. We've already been talking through the whole system at length."

Dave's gaze shifts to Maria. "What is the promise?"

Eyes wide with sincerity, Maria looks at Dave. "My dad says our promise incorporates your success system, Uncle Dave. You've taught us to hire to your success profile, develop for performance and succession, and retain the best people with engagement. We wanted to say it in a way that everyone would immediately understand and be inspired by it."

Dave looks plaintively from Maria to Mike. "Is either one of you going to tell me the promise?"

"It's *our* promise, Uncle Dave," Maria says warmly, smiling up at Mike. "It's the promise from our family to every employee. It's very simple: **No one will value you, care for you, develop you, and treat you with more respect than Stillwell Distributors.** My dad says that every action our company's leaders take is evaluated to be sure each one is consistent with that promise."

Dave nods and smiles. "'No one will value you, care for you, develop you, and treat you with more respect.' Now *that's* a promise worth making!"

For 118 years, AAIM has helped thousands of organizations, large and small, with scalable solutions to a myriad of business challenges. For more information on how we can help your company develop your promise and simplify your people processes, please contact us at:

AAIM Employers' Association
1600 S. Brentwood Boulevard
Suite #400
St. Louis, MO 63144

Web: aaimea.org
Email: info@aaimea.org
Main: 314-968-3600
Toll Free: 800-948-5700

Follow us!
Facebook: www.facebook.com/aaimea
Twitter: @AAIM_Employers
LinkedIn: AAIM Employers' Association
YouTube: AAIM Employers' Association

ACKNOWLEDGEMENTS

On behalf of all of us at the AAIM Employers' Association, I want to convey a heartfelt "thank you" to all of the organizations we serve. You share the intimacy of your businesses with us, you tell us about your triumphs and your challenges, and you place great trust in our team to help you improve and grow your business.

AAIM has enjoyed the opportunity to work with innumerable executives, business owners, and managers for over a century. These leaders have all shared the same confusion, frustration, discouragement—and yes, even the anger—that Mike Stillwell experienced in this story.

We are so grateful and proud to work with all of you – and we are honored to be your valued business partner! And, just like Dave Stillwell, we've shared in the elation Mike experienced when he applied what he had learned and began to see dramatic changes in the bottom-line business results. We sincerely hope for opportunities to continue to serve you in the years ahead and to establish new relationships with companies around the world.

I would like to thank our wonderful board of directors. Your business acumen, critical thinking skills, and openness, have fueled my desire to succeed and guide the organization. I am extremely proud to carry the AAIM torch on your behalf!

In addition, I want to thank my amazing staff! Each day, you inspire me to be a better leader! I am richly blessed to be surrounded by the ultimate team of professionals who demonstrate such a high degree of passion, energy, and dedication. You make our organization better. I have learned much from you and I look forward to our continued journey together!

A very special thank you goes to Tim Sater, AAIM's Vice President of Marketing, for your guidance and countless hours spent on this project. Team work takes dream work!

To my friend Jack Lannom, you are such a positive force! I cannot thank you enough for encouraging me to write this book! You are as wise as you are kind!

Most of all, I want to thank my wife, Angie; sons, Dominic and Joshua; daughter, Maria; my two brothers; and of course, my parents. Your love and support allow me to impart my passion for leadership with others. You serve as my foundation and I am forever grateful for having you in my life. I love you more!

Phil

About the Author

Phil Brandt, President and CEO, AAIM Employers' Association, has 25+ years of experience in working with business owners, executives, and operational leadership teams in both domestic and global business environments. Throughout his career, Phil has focused on generating sustainable profits by maximizing the output of people systems. He brings a unique blend of strategic, but practical solutions to the business world.

Phil has held senior leadership roles at several large, international organizations such as; Patriot Coal, GKN Aerospace, and Nestle Purina PetCare.

CPSIA information can be obtained
at www.ICGtesting.com
Printed in the USA
FFOW05n2117031016

9 781595 945969